LAZING ON A SUNDAY CRAFTERNOON

Little projects for people with just a little time and a little skill

Eliza Muldoon

ALLEN&UNWIN

SYDNEY•MELBOURNE•AUCKLAND•LONDON

First published in 2013

Allen & Unwin
Sydney, Melbourne, Auckland, London

83 Alexander Street
Crows Nest NSW 2065
Australia
Phone: (61 2) 8425 0100
Fax: (61 2) 9906 2218
Email: info@allenandunwin.com
Web: www.allenandunwin.com

Cataloguing-in-Publication details are available from the National Library of Australia
www.trove.nla.gov.au

ISBN 978 1 74237 865 7

Internal design by Liz Seymour
Set in 10.5/16 pt Scala by Midland Typesetters
Printed in China by South China Printing Co.

10 9 8 7 6 5 4 3 2 1

LAZING ON A SUNDAY
CI AFTERNOON

For our wonderfully inspiring Lotte May

CONTENTS

INTRODUCTION

As a youngster I found myself compulsively crafting. I didn't call it crafting then, I just called it making stuff. Making stuff was an incredibly important part of my childhood—from watching my mum hand make things to decorate my bedroom, to doing arts activities during an extended hospital stay, attending youth club holiday arts programs, and just sitting around with my friends and making the hair decorations du jour (it was the 80s, forgive me). Despite my love of making stuff I found that the older I got the less I made. At uni I did some dodgy decorating, but that was about it. Eventually, I virtually stopped making things.

Relatively recently two things made me realise that I needed to start making stuff again. The first was having a gorgeous child, Lotte, and wanting her to have the same creative memories and basic skills as I did. I wanted her to feel the joy of making stuff (especially together) and the satisfaction of creating something herself rather than buying it. The second was lecturing on the extensive benefits of art-making for our wellbeing and realising that this was an important part of my wellbeing that I had neglected.

All of this led to the development of Sunday crafternoons. I realised that I needed to make time in our week for craft or it wouldn't happen, so we set aside Sunday afternoons to make something simple and sweet. The projects needed to be short enough to keep a toddler's attention (usually about 30 minutes) and simple enough so the day remained a joy rather than became a chore. The crafternoons became an escape from my hectic week and certainly made our life a little better (and my stress levels lower). They also made our home lovelier!

There are so many things about our crafternoons that I love, but the thing that keeps me inspired (perhaps more than anything else) is when Lotte walks through the house or gets dressed in the morning or plays with her toys and says, 'You made this for me!' and then recounts the story of that day. I just love it.

SUPPLIES

Gathering craft supplies has become almost as much fun as crafting!

We regularly visit garage sales and second-hand shops looking for possible materials. Sometimes we have an idea of what we want to make, other times we just wander and see what we find.

When we started our Sunday crafternoons I was buying everything that I thought might be useful one day. It wasn't a great idea and I ended up with a massive oversupply of bits and pieces that I didn't really need. I am much more discerning now.

Re-use organisations

These are such a brilliant idea. They are essentially initiatives that collect or distribute items that might otherwise be landfill and make them available to creative people at friendly prices— sometimes free. We get so many of our crafternoon supplies through these organisations: timber offcuts, reams of paper, ribbons, buttons, corks, fabric, cotton and even our jars for storage. Our favourites are Reverse Garbage, The Bower Coop and Freecycle. Not every town has one, but every town should!

Garage sales

I suspect I started attending garage sales with my parents soon after I was born. There is so much I love about our garage sale ritual. Friday nights we'll go through the listings and choose what garage sales we'll go to and what our route will be. When we're there we will see people that we have been seeing at garage sales for the last 35 years and chat while wandering around or flicking through table contents. I often have a list of things that I would like and continue to be surprised that I typically find them. On a recent visit home to see my mum, my garage sale list included small doilies, curtain fabric, glass preserving jars, a retro clock, a blender and a pushbike. I found them all! Amazing. Without exception we always find something unexpected and inspiring too.

Op shops

I feel rather fortunate to live within easy walking distance of five op shops. At least twice a month the little one and I will go op-shopping, looking for things we need and discovering things we don't really need. Old things appeal to me aesthetically, sustainably, financially and creatively. I also like the wandering. To keep the little one involved she has a budget of $1 to spend each time we go on our op-shop tour, on the understanding that she has to donate toys back when her baskets are full—which she always does without any fuss. My favourite op shops continue to be those in country towns, and on road trips we will often stop at any we see along the way.

Council collections

These are called different things in cities all over the world, such as kerbside collection, hard garbage day, and so on. I hadn't experienced them until I moved to Sydney and I couldn't believe how much stuff was just sitting on the streets for free—a delightful treasure hunt. When I saw the trucks in action I realised they didn't take it to a wonderful re-use centre, as I had assumed—they just crushed it. Arghhhh! Destroyed forever! So now I think of it not only as a treasure hunt but also as a way to save things from the beastly crusher. Note: check that it is legal to gather goods this way where you live.

Etsy

Etsy is overflowing with wonders. This online marketplace specialises in handmade and vintage wares as well as art and craft supplies. It is also where I buy some rather cute craft goodies that I just can't get here in the Blue Mountains. Not everything we use is second-hand; things that I buy new from Etsy suppliers include string, boxes and pompoms. I tend to buy from them just a couple of times a year so the arrival of those packages is *so exciting*. My favourite suppliers also include little handwritten notes wishing me well in my crafting.

eBay

How great is eBay?! There are things that I just can't find anywhere else. Corks by the hundreds, a massive selection of vintage fabrics and bags of scrap fabrics are recent favourite discoveries. It helps to know what you are looking for though, as it can be utterly overwhelming. And you could go broke buying eBay bargains. I'm now much better at resisting the many, many temptations and staying focused on what I need. I also suggest looking around as the prices can vary a lot.

Newsagents

I buy quite a few things from local newsagents. They aren't always the cheapest option, but I like the fact that I'm supporting local business and the quality is usually reliable. They also stock wonderful things like chalk, paint, textas, ink pads and interiors magazines—such things are always found at our house.

Hardware stores

My dad was a builder so I have always felt at home in hardware stores. Dad had an enormous, well-stocked work shed that had countless bits and pieces—each with a place and a purpose. I know a lot of these things by sight but I have no idea what they are called, so I quite often head to hardware stores with a drawing or very vague description of what I need a part to do. I recently asked for a 'small metal thing that has three sides at 90-degree angles and little holes in it for screws'. I have been blessed with helpful, patient staff who will work it out with me. Often hardware stores will cut things to size for you and willingly share their experience about whether your ideas can work. Over the years both my mum and Mr Muldoon have bought me power tools and hardware supplies for birthdays and Christmas—bless them.

Friends and family

When I first started our Sunday crafternoons and told people about them, so many lovely people gave us so many lovely things. Fellow crafty mum Rachel shared some amazing Freecycle fabric with us. Karina, an artist and our neighbour and babysitter, gave us boxes full of goodies when she moved overseas. My mum and mother-in-law gave us an all-access pass to their stashes of collected goodies. The support for our little crafting adventure has been incredible, actually.

STORAGE

Good storage solutions are really important to me. I spend way more time than I should thinking about storage. We started our Sunday crafternoons while living in a little flat in the city and we didn't have much space, so storage solutions were crucial. I also like to have good storage as it makes the preparation and pack-up process so much easier. I've heard many friends say they are deterred from craft by the mess that it makes, but I've found that if there is a place for everything, then everything tends to go back in its place fairly easily.

At least four times a year I will pull out almost all my craft supplies, assess if I actually need to keep them and put them back nicely if they are keepers. It is so deeply fulfilling.

I have realised over the years that a few things typify good storage in my world:

- It should be simple—I favour practical over pretty when it comes to storage.
- I should be able to easily see what's in it—so clear containers are preferred.
- Stackable storage saves so much space.
- It should be re-usable. When I do buy plastic, I hope that I can use it over and over.
- The storage options should be flexible—I use the same type of container to store frozen vegetables as I do to store tools and fabric offcuts.

My favoured storage containers are:

- Stackable clear plastic boxes in various capacities.
- Sectioned boxes—the kind that look like fishing tackle boxes.
- Wire basket drawers.
- Tin cans—ones that we have previously used for food.
- Glass jars.
- Vintage suitcases—they look gorgeous when stacked.

BASIC TECHNIQUES

Basic stitch

We use this the most. What I mean by basic stitch is just an average-length straight machine stitch. I keep it tight enough to hold well but loose enough to make it easy to unpick and start again if needed. Yep, I make that many mistakes.

Hand stitch

This is another basic straight stitch, but done by hand. The type that starts with a double knot on the wrong side of the fabric and then continues with equal-length stitches on both sides of the fabric. Kind of equal will be fine.

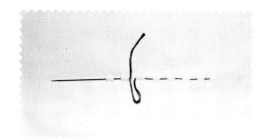

Seam allowance

I allow a seam of about 1 cm between the edge of the fabric and my stitching. It makes the calculations easy when I take the time to actually measure things and develop a pattern or plan.

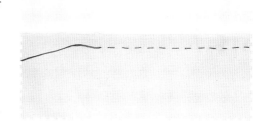

If I'm teaching a child to use a sewing machine, I use a 2 cm seam allowance—because that's what my home economics teachers taught me.

Right sides together

I almost didn't put this in here but then someone said to me, 'What do you mean right sides together?' This just means the two sides that you want the world to see when it is finished are touching each other. You almost always do this when sewing clothes.

French seam

This one actually starts with the wrong sides of the fabric together, which contradicts what I just said above. I rarely use French seams these days but when I was a time-rich, detail-oriented youngster I used them a lot, because they look lovely. You start with the wrong sides together, sew the seam close to the edge (less than 5 mm) and then trim really close to the seam. Then you turn it so the right sides are together, iron the seam flat and stitch with the standard 1 cm allowance.

When you turn it back the right way, with wrong sides together, the first seam is hidden. I now only use French seams when something should look really neat, or I am working with high-fraying fabric, or it needs a bit of extra strength (such as the '"Little Uni" Bag').

Double-folded hem

I don't always go to the trouble of finishing with a hem and when I do I only use a very basic double-folded hem. It typically involves folding 1–2 cm of fabric over and ironing it flat. Then I fold it over again and iron that flat. Finally I just stitch at the edge of the fold to hold it all together.

Templates

To me this really just means cutting out a shape and using it to make other shapes. I use templates to help me be neater; it also allows me to use the same shape over and over. I usually make them by drawing freehand onto cardboard or paper, which sometimes takes quite a bit of scribbling until I get the shape that I want. Once I am satisfied with the shape, I cut it out. You can also copy a shape that you like by tracing over the shape using translucent paper. Then you can glue the translucent paper onto cardboard and cut around them both. If I'm rushing or if it is an easy shape, I typically just cut it out of a piece of fabric that I'll be using and then use the first piece to cut subsequent pieces.

Symmetrical templates

These templates are made by folding a piece of cardboard in half and drawing half the desired shape upon the fold of the cardboard, so that when you open the cardboard you end up with the full image. I have used this method to create symmetrical hearts, triangles and monsters during our crafternoons.

Threading elastic or ribbon

I used to do this for my mum when I was really young. She would stitch the waistband or seams and then put the biggest safety pin she could find onto the end of the elastic or ribbon and I would spend an eternity pushing it through. I'd stick out my tongue in pure concentration as I went—a trait I have passed on to my little one.

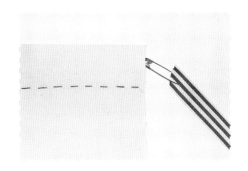

Gathering

I have done a lot of gathering this last year. Though my method continues to be rather basic, I have got faster. I simply knot the thread at the start, do a loose hand stitch, then I very carefully hold the thread tight at the untied end and pull the fabric back along the thread. I move the gathering around a bit until it's even and I'm happy with it, then I knot the loose end to secure it.

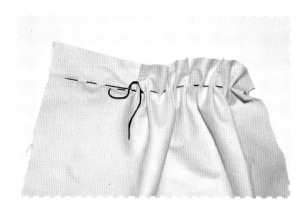

Stuffing

I use whatever I have on hand, ranging from scraps of fabric to old pillows to cotton balls, but my preference is for quality lump-free, purpose-made craft stuffing. There are a lot of options, the cheapest option being polyester; more expensive, higher quality and more eco-friendly options include Kapok and organic wool. I have bought most of mine from garage sales and op shops but you can find them at online marketplaces like Etsy and eBay as well. When stuffing things, I pull apart the stuffing to reduce the lumps and make sure I fill every little part of the object. Sometimes I will pull it all out and start again if it doesn't look right.

Vliesofix

This is great stuff. Also called 'Bondaweb', it's a double-sided adhesive web and makes any kind of appliqué easier. Before you use it, make sure any surfaces that you don't want it to adhere to (including the ironing board) are covered with nonstick paper—kitchen baking paper works well. I also make sure the iron never actually touches the Vliesofix. To use it for appliqué, draw your shape or motif on the smooth side of the Vliesofix and then cut it out. Place the rough side of the Vliesofix onto the wrong side of your fabric. Iron it on by placing nonstick paper over the top and pressing firmly without steam for 5–10 seconds. Remove the smooth paper and place the exposed adhesive onto the other piece of fabric. Then again place some nonstick paper over the top and iron it on, pressing firmly. Make sure you read the manufacturer's instructions too and follow those if they differ from mine.

Staple gun

I love being a staple gun owner. I mostly use it for stretching canvas or upholstering furniture, both of which involve stretching fabric over wood. Years ago when I was working in an art supplies store I was shown the greatest technique for effectively stretching fabric over wood (thanks Simon!). You start by laying the wood or frame on the wrong side of the fabric. Once you are sure the placement is right, you fold over one side and put a staple in the back centre, securing the fabric to the wood. Then go to the opposite side and pull the fabric firmly over the back and put a staple in the centre. You then do the other two sides the same way, pulling the fabric firmly and putting one staple in the centre. Go around each of the sides and pull fabric as firmly as you can and staple the remainder of each side, one by one. It is a really quick and effective method. I've used this method to cover stools, our kitchen chairs and every stretched canvas in our house.

Blanket stitch

This is such a beautiful stitch. I can remember the moment I first saw it when I was a little girl. I spent years trying to work out how to do it. It is quite time-consuming but certainly worth the effort. This is how I do it. You stitch from left to right, bringing the needle from back to front at A. Then you insert your needle from the front to the back and then to the front again in a single motion at B and C. Before you pull your needle through the fabric, make sure you place the thread under the point of your needle, as shown in the picture.

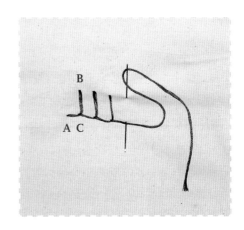

The basic kit

Having a good set of well-ordered basic supplies makes crafting so much more delightful. It means that if we have an idea we can usually make it without having to go anywhere or buy anything new. The items in my basic kit are easy to find and inexpensive, except the sewing machine—but I actually managed to get that for free too! You could put together your own basic kit without going to much effort at all. You probably have most of it already.

- Black and white thread (I like having other colours on hand too).
- Needles.
- Pins.
- Scissors.
- Measuring tape and ruler.
- Quick unpick.
- Sewing machine.
- Crochet or embroidery thread.
- Rope.
- Ribbons.
- Fabric bits and pieces.
- A4 felt sheets.
- Coloured and patterned paper.
- Magazines and cut-out images.
- Glue—glue stick and strong all-purpose glue.
- Vliesofix/Bondaweb—double-sided iron-on adhesive web.

1 Colour-coded collage card

Idea and inspiration

Colour-coding, collage and handmade gift cards are three of my favourite craft activities. Bringing them together is an absolute delight.

It's actually quite hard to calculate the total time taken because I can spend hours browsing through magazines! However, these images were all from two magazines so it didn't take too long for this project. It was also difficult to limit this to just one afternoon. Even now I'm tempted to start flicking through magazines.

Time taken Less than 10 minutes for each card

What we used

- Magazine pictures
- Scissors
- A4 white cardboard
- Glue stick for each person

What I did

First the preparation

- Lotte and I sat down on the floor with magazines and looked for lovely pictures. For me, the keys to a good picture are: it doesn't have any type on it, it is front on, I can see the whole object, and it is the right size for the card. Home decor is my preferred genre and my choices tend to be furniture; Lotte's tend to be animals.
- Once we made our selection, I loosely cut out everything we liked from the magazines and sorted the pictures into colour categories as we went. Little thought was given to the construction and card design at this stage.

Now for the construction

- I folded a sheet of cardboard in half (top to bottom) then half again. If you are using thick cardboard, cutting the A4 page in half and folding once would be better.
- Then I trimmed the chosen images as closely as I could and started arranging the images for each card. I tried not to overthink it, relying on the common colour to make it look cohesive, and just moved things around until I was happy with it. I would often try quite a few combinations before settling on my final image.
- I put the glue on the back of the images and carefully stuck them onto the front of the card. The glue should be dry by the time you finish your next card.
- Repeat to create as many cards as time allows—I could do this all day!

Variations

- There are so many picture possibilities—I'm itching to make more right now!
- Smaller versions also make gorgeous gift tags.
- Sometimes I wrap gifts in plain or brown paper and stick the collage directly onto the package wrapping.

2 Basic ring bling

I have seen many button rings over the years. I have bought some, and lost some as well. I wanted to make a nice big black button ring for myself to wear to work, but I didn't have any of the metal ring backs that they're typically glued onto. I tried a few things and then found some hat elastic. Brilliant. It works a treat and is quite a comfortable fit too.

Time taken 10 minutes

What we used

- Button
- Cotton spool, to help with threading
- Black hat elastic

What I did

First the preparation

- Obviously, I chose the button—it had to have holes big enough for the hat elastic. I quite like large rings so the bigger the button, the better. I also prefer buttons with four holes but two-holed buttons also work.
- I found something about the same width as my finger (I used a little cotton spool—a stick would work as well).

Now for the construction

- I threaded the elastic through two diagonal holes in the button and wrapped it around the spool.
- Then I threaded it back through the other diagonal holes and made another loop of elastic.
- Finally I tied a tight and discreet little knot under the button. I cut the elastic close to the knot and my ring was done.

Variations

- A similar method could be used to make hair elastics. I would just use a two-holed button and thread the hat elastic through the holes, then tie a knot.
- You could also, of course, buy the metal ring backs—this will hugely expand the range of buttons and things you can make into rings. Old earrings, tiny flowers and little plastic animals all come to mind.

AND THE LITTLE ONE

This was made quite quickly—I spent most of the ten minutes working out how to tie it—so Lotte simply asked what I was doing, watched a little and that was it. I thought she wasn't paying much attention until later when she made one by herself and brought it over to me to tie the knot. So proud!

3 Board of corks

Idea and inspiration

I can't explain how excited I was when I saw a bucketload of wine corks for sale at my much-loved re-use centre. When I was a kid, I saw a board made of corks in a magazine and I wondered how anyone would ever collect enough corks to make one (my mum was a non-drinker and my dad was more of a beer or rum man). I actually started asking people to save them for me but I never managed to get enough. So, when I saw the glorious bucketful, I knew exactly what I would use them for. I went straight upstairs to the timber offcut section and chose a bit of wood that wouldn't need any cutting, 26 cm × 30 cm × 8 mm. Then I floated home.

If you don't collect or stumble across a pile of wine corks, you might find them online (I have since bought them on eBay too). Choosing timber that matches the length and width of the corks saves time and effort; if you can't find a suitable offcut, you can get a board cut to size at hardware stores (or look through their offcuts). They can also advise you on the best glues—you need one that's quite thick so you can apply a layer to work the cork into.

I love this board so much that I only stick one thing on it at a time—usually sweet thank you cards from students (like this one).

Time taken 30 minutes—because I didn't have to cut the timber

What we used

- About 100 wine corks
- Piece of plywood 8-mm thick
- Newspaper—it's messy!
- All-purpose glue
- Picture-hanging strips—the removable, double-sided adhesive kind

What I did

First the preparation
I worked out how many corks I needed by lining them up across the top and then down the side. I made sure they covered the edges so I couldn't see the backing board once the corks were glued on. I had six corks across and fourteen down, so 84 corks were needed in total.

Now for the construction
- I spread out newspaper and put the board on top.
- I put a line of glue across the board, enough to squish the corks into. Next I very carefully glued the cork onto the board, arranging them one at a time so I could see the images. I also thought about ensuring the ends were even so I would start to consider both the images and the size of the corks as I near the edges. It took quite a bit of focus but I got more efficient as I went on.

Note: I can't be too rough with it, I realised after I knocked a cork off while clumsily carrying the board. The cork was easily glued back on though.

4 Felt food—The egg

Idea and inspiration

I first saw these in a magazine photo where a little girl was playing with them. Not being very familiar then with the modern world of craft, I hadn't seen them before. Felt food—genius! So I did an internet search for 'felt food'. Oh my goodness! My life shifted a little that day. There are some incredible and inspirational items out there. I chose the really easy ideas. I have never actually looked up how to make them (though I probably should). So this is the way I made one of our favourites—the egg. It was also the first toy I made for my daughter.

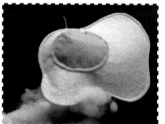

Time taken 15 minutes—some foods take less time, some more

What we used

- A4 white and yellow felt sheets
- Pencil
- Scissors
- Sewing machine—easily hand-stitched though
- Stuffing

What I did

First the preparation

- On a piece of white felt, I drew an eggwhite shape. I put another piece of white felt behind that one and cut out both pieces inside the pencil line (so the pencil marks were cut off). Cutting out both pieces together ensured they were the same.
- Then I drew a little yolk shape on the yellow felt and cut that out.

Now for the construction

- I placed the yolk somewhere egg-like on one of the eggwhite pieces and straight-stitched the yolk on, with a seam close to the edge and most of the way around. I put a little stuffing in the open section while still at the machine, before finishing the seam. I trimmed the threads as I finished each stage.
- Then I put the two white pieces together, with the yolk visible on the top, and sewed a seam quite close to the edge, most of the way around. I filled the egg with more stuffing—not too much though—and finished the seam.

Variations

- You are only limited by your imagination—and skills. We have made toast, biscuits (with little embroidered choc chips), and lettuce (which was just a wobbly cut-out of green felt). Some of these were made on a crafternoon with my talented friends Lee and Stella, who way outclassed me—all while monitoring four children in the background!
- When starting your felt food collection, try giving your children simple cut-out felt pieces to play with while you sew.

AND THE LITTLE ONE

Lotte is always eager to make suggestions for food types. Now I just get out the box of felt food and she plays with those while she waits for the new arrival. The egg continues to be a favourite though.

We bought a little old frying pan and she has now mastered the art of flipping it in the pan.

5 Good-hair-day headband

Idea and inspiration

I have been making these since I was about ten, maybe younger. When Liberty print was cool in the 80s, I made one out of Liberty print. When paisley had a comeback in the 90s, I made one out of paisley fabric. When retro prints were cool in the . . . well, you get the idea. These headbands are my way of indulging the trend du jour without spending more than a few dollars. Oh so miserly. Another reason I love them so much is because they can work wonders on a bad hair day. And I have many, many bad hair days.

I am *very* happy with this one—it is such a gorgeous print! This was a beautiful Japanese fabric square from a craft fair: I bought it after convincing myself I would make a patchwork quilt (as if) and it had been lying around unused for two years. I also think this headband is the best fit so far—thanks to the elastic, either of us can wear it.

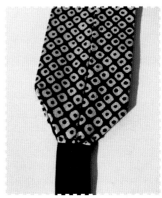

Time taken 30 minutes, or less once you have the hang of it

What we used

- Measuring tape
- Fabric piece—60 × 20 cm is plenty
- Scissors
- Sewing machine—could be hand-sewn too
- An iron
- Spray starch (optional)
- Piece of elastic about 3–4 cm long
- Needle and thread

What I did

First the preparation

- To work out the fabric length, I measured around my head where the headband would go (53 cm).
- After deciding how wide I wanted my headband to be (5 cm), I doubled the width and added a 1 cm seam allowance for each side (total width 12 cm).
- I cut my fabric to size (53 × 12 cm). I didn't need a seam allowance on the ends (for reasons that will become clear).

Now for the construction

- I folded the fabric in half lengthways with the right sides together, and did a basic straight stitch along the open side. (Hand-sewing with a basic straight stitch would work too.)

- After turning the fabric right side out—it looked like a tube of fabric—I ironed it flat with the seam down the middle of one side. You can starch it at this point, if you like.
- At the ironing board, I also folded each of the ends into a triangle and ironed them, before tucking the ends of the triangle (about 1 cm) inside the tube.
- Then I inserted the piece of elastic between the ends so about 2 cm of elastic was visible, and hand-stitched (rather badly) the elastic and fabric ends together. (With hindsight I realised that a sewing machine may have made more sense here.) I neatly trimmed all threads.
- The headband was now finished and ready to wear.

Note: If the headband doesn't fit properly, just unstitch one end and increase or decrease the length of the elastic—not a big deal (I'm quite used to undoing and redoing now).

Variations

These headbands can be thinner, wider, adorned with flowers, embroidered—whatever you like! You can also create a more 50s look by making another little rectangle of fabric and tying a knot around the top of the headband.

AND THE LITTLE ONE

I had a lot of fabric out for this project, so Lotte simply played one of her favourite games—'stepping stones'. Fabric pieces were spread around the room and she had to stay on them so the 'water monster' didn't get her. We have found this game works much better on floors that aren't too slippery!

6 Loving letters

Idea and inspiration

This was inspired by the purchase of a roll of self-adhesive magnetic tape at a stationery store. My thought process went something like this:

Magnetic tape! Genius! I need this!
Hmmm. What can I make with magnetic tape?
Pretty much limited to stuff that will stick on the fridge.
What would I want on the fridge?
Letters to make words! Maybe I can use them to teach the little one too.

Magnetic tape *is* genius. I did need it.

Time taken About an hour

What we used

- Magnetic tape
- Ruler
- Pencil
- White cardboard—20 × 21 cm
- Black marker—width of choice
- Eraser
- Quick laminate sheets
- Paper cutter or scissors

What I did

First the preparation

- To determine the width of my letters, I measured the width of the magnetic tape (2 cm). Then I drew a 2 cm × 3 cm grid in pencil on the sheet of cardboard.
- I looked up Scrabble tile letter allocation to help me decide how many I should have of each letter. I decided to have three of each vowel and two of each consonant.
- Using pencil first, I wrote a letter in each rectangle of the grid. I went over them in black marker pen, before erasing any sign of my pencilled letters (I love erasing).

Now for the construction

- To help the letters last longer, I stuck a sheet of laminate on the front of each cardboard sheet. This is done by placing the adhesive side onto the lettered side of the cardboard.
- I cut the sheets into 2-cm wide strips of letters—this made it easy to stick the magnetic tape on the back.
- Finally I cut out each letter.

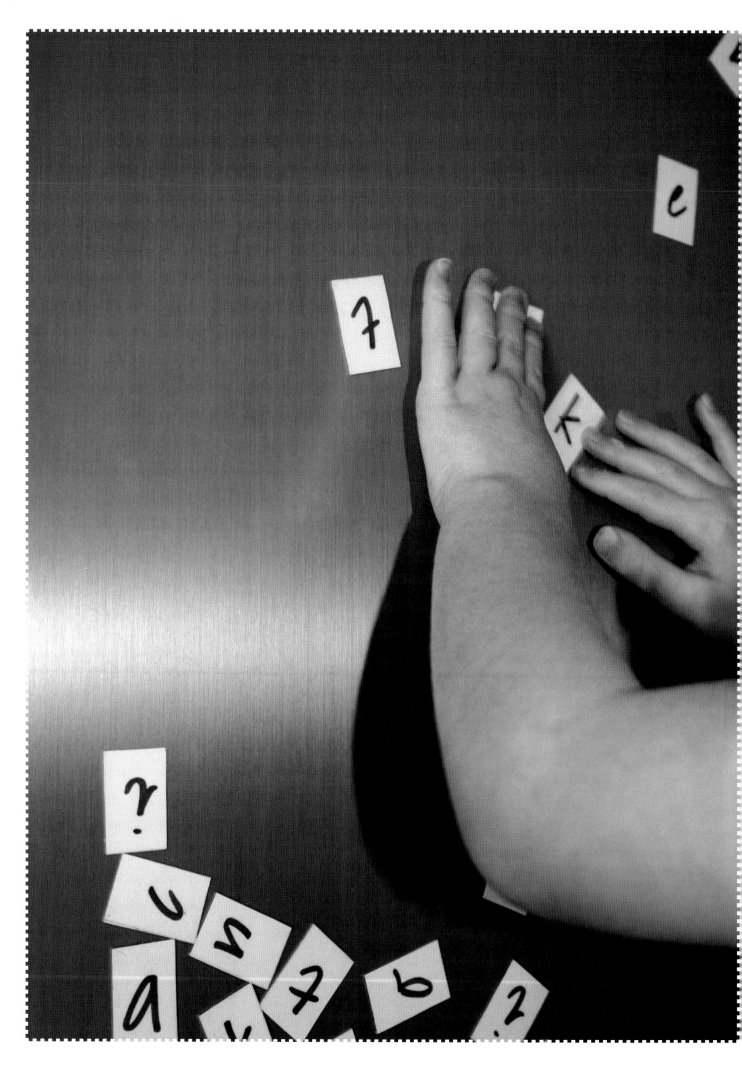

Variations

- Instead of writing them, you could type and print out the letters.
- I think these would be even cuter in children's handwriting (mine can't write yet though).
- You could make the vowels a different colour, or make all the letters various colours. Try using coloured paper, or even white letters on black paper. (Oh, I wish I'd done that now!)
- If you can't get the tape, you can use A4 magnetic sheets and then trim them to size—these are also available from stationery stores.

AND THE LITTLE ONE

This was when my daughter first discovered the joy of ruling lines.
She didn't stick it out for the whole process, but was happy for me to
continue uninterrupted, except for cuddles and chats.
The letters have been used to make lots of little phrases, like 'we love you'
and 'welcome' for guests. I really look forward to the day when Lotte
starts making her own words with them.

7 Oh-so-simple skirt

Idea and inspiration

My friend Deb's mum made me a hot-pink tube skirt in the 80s and I wore it until it fell apart. While tripping down memory lane one day, it occurred to me that I now have the straight-stitch skills I need to make such skirts (well, very basic imitations of them). Woohoo!

These are fantastic preschool skirts. My daughter now has five of them.

Time taken 30 minutes is plenty of time

What we used

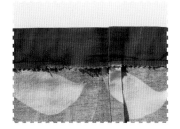

- Measuring tape
- Fabric—bought at a re-use centre
- Thick elastic—I just used elastic I found at home (it was from post–knee surgery stockings!)
- Sewing machine
- Big safety pin

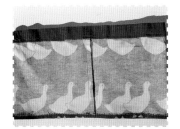

What I did

First the preparation

- I measured around Lotte's waist and added 20 cm (it seemed like a reasonable amount—enough for seam allowance, a nice gather as well as a little room for growth. I would add about 30–50 cm for me though).
- Then I measured the desired length and to that I added 10 cm to allow for elastic and seams.
- My fabric ended up about 70 cm × 35 cm. The width was double the length. (I'm going to use that ratio from now on.)
- To decide on the length of the elastic, I just wrapped it around her waist, stretching it a little. When I've added the seams, that's usually sufficient to hold it tight.

Now for the construction

- I made this in the easiest possible way. First, I folded the fabric in half widthways with the right sides facing and sewed a side seam in a basic straight stitch.
- Then I just folded over the top, leaving enough room for a seam and the elastic. As the skirt won't be stretching much at the waist, I just used a normal straight stitch for this seam—use a stretch stitch if you think it will need to stretch around the waist. I left a gap in the seam big enough to thread the elastic through.
- I put a big safety pin in one end of the elastic to help me thread it. I was really careful not to twist the elastic (I've made that mistake before).
- After removing the safety pin, I sewed the two ends of the elastic together. I didn't finish the gap in the seam—this means I can adjust the elastic without fuss later if needed.

- I don't always hem the bottom of the skirt, but you might want to—if so, a double-folded hem would suffice (see the 'Basic techniques' section). I turned the skirt the right way out, and that was it.

Variations

- I have made these skirts out of stretch and non-stretch fabric—both work well.
- A recent discovery is that I can make these skirts out of singlets and T-shirts I no longer wear, mostly because they are damaged or misshapen. I tend to leave the T-shirt or singlet whatever width it is, cut off the top of it, sew a waistband and just add elastic.
- The most recent skirt was made out of a vintage embroidered table runner. I urgently needed to make a skirt for a school 'dress in yellow day' and it was the only yellow fabric I had on hand. Lotte looks like vintage sunshine when she wears it!

AND THE LITTLE ONE

Lotte seemed amazed—it was only the second time I had ever made her clothes and I don't think she had thought much before this about how clothes are made. She very happily stayed with me for measuring and watched over my shoulder for constructing. It was all so quick.

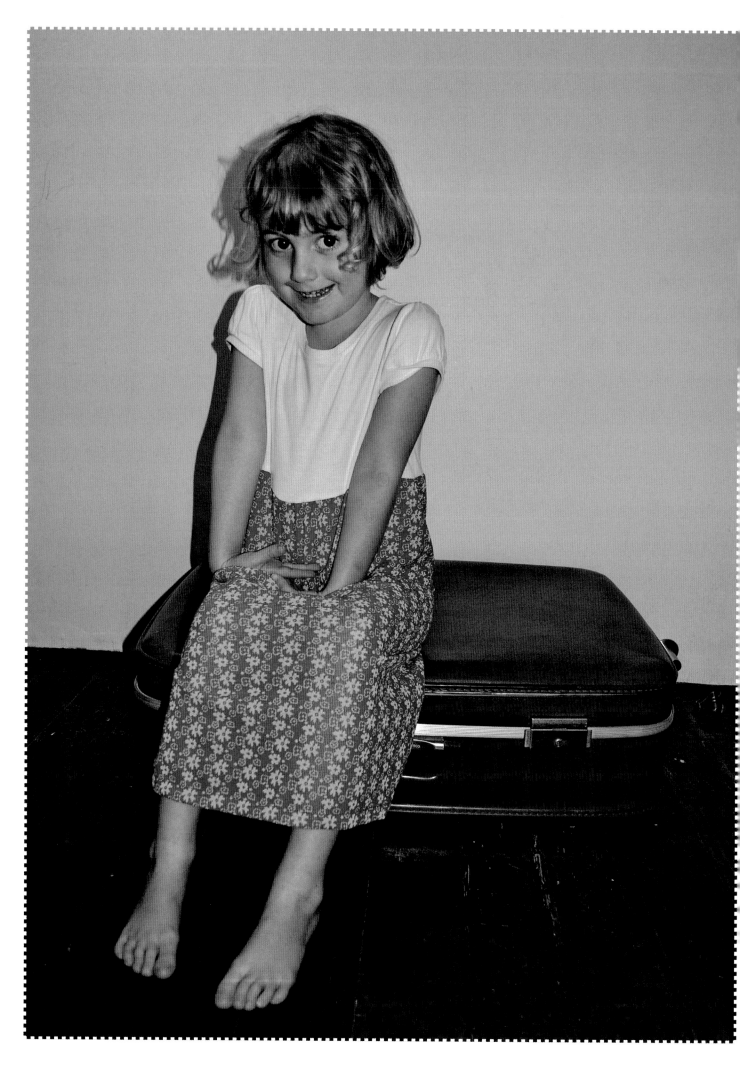

8 Cheap cheat's dress

Idea and inspiration

This was completely inspired by a little girl we saw at the park who was wearing a pretty dress with a white top and coloured, tiered ruffles on the bottom. 'I could make that,' I thought. I imagined creating tiers of gorgeous vintage fabric . . . but then I acknowledged my limitations and settled on this easier option. I love this idea though, and we've since made quite a few of them.

Time taken 30 minutes (I get faster every time)

What we used

- Cheap department store T-shirt—bought on sale!
- Pen
- Scissors
- Pins
- Measuring tape
- Piece of vintage fabric—I have no idea where it came from
- Sewing machine

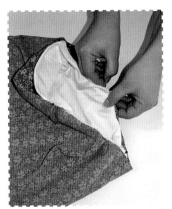

What I did

First the preparation

- I put the T-shirt on Lotte and marked with pen where to cut it—I settled on a little higher than her belly button, then I cut it.
- After cutting it, I folded the T-shirt in half sideways and put four pins in to make reference points, one on each side seam, one in the middle of the front and one in the middle of the back.
- To determine the size of the vintage bottom fabric, I put the t-shirt back on her and measured the length from the cut t-shirt edge to her ankles (adding a seam allowance at the top and bottom)—this was 50 cm. To work out the width, I measured around the base of the T-shirt and added 20 cm. Make sure you jot down the measurements—I think I'll remember them, but I usually don't! Then I cut the fabric to size.

Now for the construction

- With right sides facing, I folded the vintage fabric in half widthways, and stitched a seam. I now had a tube of fabric. The seam that I just stitched will be centred at the back of the dress.
- I folded the fabric in half, like I did with the T-shirt, and marked quarters in pencil—one on each side, one in the middle of the front and one in the seam at the middle of the back.
- I slipped the trimmed, pinned T-shirt upside-down into the fabric so that the right sides of the T-shirt and fabric were together and the seam was in the centre at the back of the T-shirt.

- One at a time, I matched the pinned T-shirt quarters with the marked fabric quarters and re-pinned them together. They were different sizes so it looked a bit wrong at this stage.
- To sew them together, I put a couple of little basic straight stitches at the first pin and, holding both pieces just before the next pin, I stretched the T-shirt until it matched the fabric evenly and then sewed that whole quarter. I then continued to sew the next quarter in the same way, and so on.
- To finish, I hemmed the bottom. (Though I only did this after I found out that you would see it!) I trimmed all the threads, turned the dress the right way out and I was done.

Note: I would suggest using a suitable stitch for jersey fabric. I don't though, and it always seems to work out.

Variations

- You can make them any length—shorter dresses have been better since the little one started climbing like a monkey. Grown-up versions work too!
- Instead of a T-shirt, you could use a singlet; you can also make this dress using a coloured or patterned top.

9 Beautiful bunch of buttons

Idea and inspiration

My mum had a collection of buttons from generations of family clothes—the days when clothes were worn until they could be worn no more, and after that the buttons would be cut off for future use and the fabric recycled for rags or to make other things. When I was a child I loved sorting the buttons by various themes.

I love these old family buttons. I wanted to make a little display out of them and frame it, but couldn't work out how. Then I thought, 'Cross-stitch frame!' Round things in a round frame—great.

If you don't happen to belong to generations of women who collected buttons, you can buy bags of mixed buttons from craft stores or online. The cross-stitch frame was bought at a garage sale, but these are also available at craft suppliers. I used a piece of leftover canvas that I was given for Christmas in about 1995. The thread I chose contrasted with the buttons and matched the fabric; a less visible thread might be better depending on your design.

Time taken About an hour (less for the actual construction)

What we used
- Buttons
- Cross-stitch frame
- Canvas
- Needle and thread

What we did

First the preparation
- I chose my buttons and played around with the arrangement (this took most of the hour because I got side-tracked by memories), and ended up with seven buttons of varying sizes and textures in earthy tones.
- To work out the size of the fabric, I put the frame on the canvas and traced around the outside of the circle. I cut the canvas, allowing about 5 cm extra for framing it.

Now for the construction
- I stretched the fabric into the cross-stitch frame. I had never used one before but it was easy to work out: I put the fabric over the inner circle, pushed the outer circle over that, and tightened the outer circle enough to hold it together. Then I started pulling the fabric taut, gradually tightening the outer circle as well. I worked evenly from opposite sides until the fabric was tight as a drum (but not so tight that the frame warped).

- Then I replicated the button arrangement onto the fabric. I just sewed one button at a time, leaving the others where they were (on the floor). I used a neat stitch at the front to sew the button on and hid all the messy stitching at the back, trimming threads as much as possible as I went.
- Once the buttons were on, I sewed a quick big straight stitch around the edge of the fabric, using it to gather the fabric and keep it hidden at the back.

Variations

- Oh so many—I could make dozens of these! Instead of canvas, you could use patterned fabric, embroidered serviettes or doilies.
- The frame could be filled with buttons, or use the buttons to make shapes like hearts or circles. Or you could try buttons of different sizes and shapes in one colour—I think I'll do a red theme next.

AND THE LITTLE ONE

We were both very excited making this project. I started trying to make a heart shape out of similar-sized buttons but my arrangement just wasn't working. The final design was actually much closer to Lotte's ideas. She very happily continued sorting and arranging buttons while I stitched. Then she got a small wheelbarrow, put the buttons in it and wandered about the house for a while, before selling the buttons back to me. It was the first time she said, 'We made this together.' Heart. Melted.

10 Dutiful denim bag

Idea and inspiration

This project was totally inspired by the purchase of some bamboo handles on a visit to the Blue Mountains (the visit that made me want to move here). I actually went home with two huge bags of op-shop delights that sparked off many projects. The first thing I used were these handles. I decided they'd feature in a bag that was simple and practical—I needed it to hold a laptop and some files—and this fits that description well. I have used this bag so often and it still looks sturdy and quite sweet.

Handles like these can be bought new from fabric and craft stores or online. The denim came from a 1-metre length I bought at a re-use centre—it matched my handles nicely and was the strongest fabric I had on hand.

Time taken About an hour, I think—I did it in two shifts

What we used
- Piece of denim
- Pencil or chalk
- Ruler
- Scissors
- Bamboo handles
- Sewing machine
- An iron
- Pins

What I did
First the preparation
- Because the bag was for a laptop and some files that I store in a plastic sleeve, I just put the plastic sleeve on the fabric and drew around it. Leaving enough for a seam allowance and to allow for the thickness of the laptop, I ruled a rectangle around the outside of my drawn line on one piece of denim and cut it out.
- Then I placed the first rectangle on another bit of denim and used it as a template to draw and cut a second piece. These formed the body of the bag.
- For the handles I decided to use two additional rectangles to hold them on. So I measured the length of the handles (20 cm)—this was enough to fit nicely between the ends and include a seam allowance. I then worked out how much fabric I would need to fold over the handles and attach them to the bag. I thought a visible 5 cm would look nice, so I doubled that and added a seam allowance (total width 12 cm). I cut out two rectangles, each 20 cm × 12 cm.

Now for the construction

- For the body of the bag, I put the pieces right sides together and used a tight straight stitch on three sides (leaving an opening at the top). I added a second row of stitches over the first to double the strength, because it was to hold something heavy and valuable. Overlocking and finishing seams is a good idea—but I didn't do it.
- I turned it the right way out—it already looked quite like a bag—and ironed it flat. I also ironed a double fold at the top, folding to the inside, to make it look neat and tidy. I didn't actually stitch it but you could use a double-folded-hem method to finish it if you like.
- For the handle sections, I just ironed a 1-cm seam around the edges and straight-stitched it.
- To finish the bag, I laid out all the elements on the table. I put a handle above the bag, folded a rectangle over it and pinned it into place, ensuring that the outside and inside folds were exactly the same. (I rarely use pins but needed them here to make sure both sides of the rectangle were attached.) I sewed the handle piece to the bag by sewing along the existing bottom stitching of the rectangle, making sure both the inside and outside were stitched. I then added a second row of stitches for strength. I sewed on the second handle in the same way.

Variations

There are plenty of handles available now and bags are just so easy and cheap to make. (It actually takes me less time to make a bag than it would to choose one in a shop!) The added bonus is that you can make them to your size and specifications.

- You can use the same shape and add longer fabric handles to create your own basic tote bag.
- You could add pockets on the inside or the outside.
- You could have contrasting fabrics on the front and back of the bag.
- You could even embroider it—if you are feeling particularly crafty.

AND THE LITTLE ONE

Whenever there is a ruler, pencils and scissors, my daughter is happy. She has her own scissors that I get out on such occasions. I gave her some scrap denim, some chalk and some paper and she was occupied (and messy). Lotte asked questions throughout, mainly about whether I would make her a bag soon and what would it be like, and could she take it to the beach and would it be big enough to carry a drink. The answer to all of those questions was, of course, yes.

R. d'anorlique de Boheme

R. de Galanga

Salsepareille

abique

thank you

11 Elegant envelopes and nice notecards

Idea and inspiration

My childhood penfriends would be familiar with these envelopes—I've been making them for years. I like them because all I really need is a magazine, scissors, and some cardboard and glue. Also, as I wrap gifts mainly with brown paper and string or stripy ribbon, these envelopes look lovely tucked under the bow.

My magazines of choice these days are home decor, but in adolescence they would have been some kind of teen or music magazine. These are from *World of Interiors*; I love the full-page, text-free images. If there's a little bit of text on the page, I usually stick another picture over it or try to hide it with the folding.

Time taken Just a few minutes each

What we used

- Magazine pages
- Scissors
- Glue stick or double-sided tape
- Plain white A4 cardboard
- Pen

What we did

First the preparation

- We looked through old magazines and chose a nice set of images. (For me, this part can take hours of casual browsing!) I tend to do batches in themes. In a recent batch I used trees and greenery; these ones were for thank you cards.
- I carefully tore the pages out, neatly trimming the torn side afterwards.

Now for the construction

- Really easy. I have seen more complicated folds than this, but I simply folded the page with about 40 per cent for the front, 40 per cent for the back and 20 per cent for the flap.
- On the wrong side of the centre section of the page (the front of the envelope), I put a thin strip of glue along the sides, as close to the edge as possible. (A thin strip of double-sided tape will work too.)
- I folded up the bottom section (the back of the envelope), making sure the edges met neatly. I let the glue dry and I had a cute, re-use envelope.
- For the card I always keep it simple—usually plain white or brown cardboard. I just cut an A4 piece of cardboard in thirds, trimming the edges if necessary to fit in the envelope.
- I drew around this card the way I used to in the 90s. One colleague suggested I had some kind of compulsive box-drawing condition because I even drew borders on Post-its.

Variations

- You can make these envelopes in various sizes and fold them in all sorts of ways. You can create a template by undoing any envelope that you have and tracing around it onto your magazine page. Then you just fold it into shape and glue it accordingly. The fold I've used requires the least effort and thought.
- Recently I have made some envelopes with stitching instead of glue.
- I have some gorgeous old children's books that I made into party packs for a friend's daughter's party. They were essentially just envelopes that I filled with notebooks and little packs of coloured pencils.
- I am considering writing little messages under the flap of the envelope as a surprise.

12 Little apron

Idea and inspiration

I have been lucky enough to find a few cute vintage aprons lately. I only need them once a year when I teach art as therapy, but when I see a hand-embroidered and trimmed apron in an op shop for 80 cents, how can I just leave it there? I haven't found any kids' ones though, so I thought I would make an apron for my daughter. There do seem to be a lot of little aspiring chefs around at the moment.

I love dress-ups and how easily kids can put on an apron and spend the next half hour preparing food, or how they put on 'Janey socks' and break into dance moves. I try putting on tracksuit pants in the hope that it will inspire me to exercise—maybe one day.

Time taken 45 minutes

What we used

- Fabric for the apron—this was a 1-m square piece left over from Christmas gift-wrapping
- Small piece of fabric for a pocket
- An iron
- Sewing machine
- Needle and thread
- Measuring tape
- Ribbon—enough to go around the recipient and tie a bow at the back

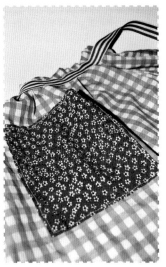

What I did

First the preparation

- To work out the size of the apron, I measured loosely around Lotte's hips to decide the width; I wanted it to go a bit past her knees so that was the length. I settled on 85 cm wide × 35 cm long, and cut the fabric to size.
- I chose a 10-cm square piece from my patchwork square stash for the pocket.

Now for the construction

- First, I ironed a hem on all four sides of the apron, and sewed the hem using a basic straight stitch.
- Then I ironed a hem on the four sides of the patchwork square, but only stitched one side of the square. This became the top of the pocket. I stitched the pocket to the apron on the remaining three sides. I just guessed where to put it. (No surprises that it was off-centre!)

- Across the top of the apron, just below the seam, I sewed a very loose straight stitch by hand and gathered it. I wanted the gathered width to go just around Lotte's hips, but by this stage she'd run off so I just guessed. It worked though.
- Finally, I sewed the ribbon across the gathering, hiding the white stitch on the white stripe. I left a bit of the gathering visible at the top because I thought it looked sweet.

Variations

- You can make it less flouncy by just folding three pleats at the top instead of gathering it. To do this just fold about 5 cm or so at the centre of the fabric and then add two more folds halfway along either side.
- You could add vertical seams from the bottom to the top of the pocket to make smaller sections that could happily hold little utensils.
- You could make an apron in this way for grown-ups too—simply adjust the fabric measurements to suit.

AND THE LITTLE ONE

Lotte was involved in the fabric selection—I thought her choices were mighty cute! She didn't stick around for the sewing, though; she was already playing with her toy stove and bringing me 'baked goods'. When I gave this to her, she said, 'It's so pretty. Everyone watch me run around the kitchen table in my apron.' (Because that is what one does when one puts on an apron.)

13 My lady green sleeves

Idea and inspiration

The idea for this creation developed following a discussion with fellow mum Lee about making cheap department store clothes cute. There seems to be only one place to buy clothes for kids in our new town (not including op shops). Now I see design features on clothes and think, 'How can I remake that using a department store basic?' On this occasion I was flicking through a magazine and saw ruffles. Dozens of ideas popped into my head. This is one of them.

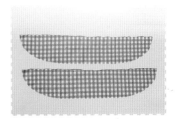

Time taken 30 minutes

What we used

- Light fabric—50 cm square would be enough
- Chalk or pencil
- Scissors
- Basic singlet top
- Sewing machine
- An iron
- Needle and thread

What I did

First the preparation

- I was making this up as I went along. I actually started with quite thick fabric but it didn't sit well, so I immediately unpicked it and decided to use the lighter gingham instead (Christmas gift-wrapping leftovers again—it'll match her apron).
- There was enough fabric to make two sleeves that were 40 cm × 20 cm. That meant the 'puff' could be about 10 cm wide, which seemed good.
- To create a tapered sleeve, I folded the fabric in half widthways and then lengthways as well. You can see the shape that I drew in the top photo (the folding ensures symmetry). I cut out the final shape.
- Placing the right sides together, I used the first piece as a template to draw the shape of the second piece—so they were vaguely similar—and cut the second piece.
- Then I cut another two pieces for the second sleeve, again using the first piece as my template so they are all the same size.

Now for the construction

- With the right sides of one sleeve together, I straight-stitched around the tapered side.
- I turned it the right way out and ironed the seam flat. Then I tucked the straight edges in and ironed them to create a neat 1-cm hem. Then I sewed both edges together using a visible machine straight stitch, making sure it was close to the edge.

- Again along the straight side, over the machine stitch, I hand-sewed a loose gather stitch. I gathered the fabric until it was 20 cm long.
- I folded the gathered piece in half and lined up the halfway point with the shoulder seam on the singlet. I would have pinned it to secure it—if I could have found my pins, that is. I stitched the sleeve to the arm hole of the singlet.
- Then I did the second sleeve the same way.

Variations

- I'm rather fond of the idea of sewing things around sleeves now—I have plans to cut doilies in half and then gather and attach them.
- Trimming the sleeve edges with pompoms would be rather cute too.
- Then I might start trimming the bottom of our homemade skirts!

14 Bathing beastie

Idea and inspiration

The little one loves a bath but isn't so fond of the washing part. Especially when it comes to getting off the afternoon's assortment of milk, jam and, at the moment, snot. So I thought I should create something to make the whole process a bit more enjoyable.

This project required very few materials. I bought the brown Christmas-themed face washer at an op shop (why was it ever made?). The embroidery cotton was left over from a cardigan repair, and the leather scraps came from a re-use centre years ago. (Apologies to my vegetarian friends—vinyl would work too!)

Time taken 30 minutes

What we used

- Face washer
- Scissors
- Marker pen
- Black embroidery thread
- Leather scraps
- Sewing machine

What I did

First the preparation

- After cutting off the Christmas embroidery, I drew around my hand to gauge the approximate size and make sure I had enough to cut out two pieces. I made the edge of the washer form the bottom of the beastie so I wouldn't have to finish any seams.
- I folded one piece in half, drew half the beastie's shape along the fold, and cut it out while still folded, so I knew the result would be symmetrical. Then I unfolded the first piece and used it as the template to cut a second piece.
- On the front of one piece I sewed some eye-like things using the black embroidery thread. I stitched them well as the beastie will go through the wash a lot. Trim the threads so they don't get caught when you put your hand in the beastie.
- I asked Lotte what kind of animal she would like—a cat. So I cut out small triangles from the leather scraps to make ears that I thought were vaguely cat-like.

Now for the construction

- I placed the two leather triangles at the top of one piece of fabric with the points facing down, then I put the other piece of fabric on top. Make sure the right sides are together if your fabric looks like it has a right side; you need to be able to see the back of your eye stitching.
- Leaving the bottom open, I sewed a tight straight stitch around the edge—a fairly small seam allowance is fine. If you have an overlocker, it would be a good idea; I didn't though and it seems to be staying together.
- I turned it the right way out, and the bathing beastie was ready for action.

Variations

I am definitely going to make more of these. I have been collecting washers and I have a white one to make a bunny and with the leftovers from this I'm going to make one that looks more like a bear. You could make any kind of animal or character you want. I think some brightly coloured beasties might be good too.

AND THE LITTLE ONE

Lotte actually watched this project rather intently from start to finish—more than usual. There weren't many parts that she could do but it came together rather quickly. The bathing beastie was certainly well received and achieves everything we hoped he would!

15 Nice and nifty notebook

Idea and inspiration

I'm hooked on stationery. Like many 80s children I coveted boxed stationery, I collected erasers and I squealed with delight when they released the mini Pacer pencil. I can still recall the first time I saw our town newsagent's counter topped with a box of white pens. As I get older the obsession continues, though it's milder these days. Admittedly I have begun carting my laptop to meetings instead of notepads—but there are some needs only a beautiful notebook can fulfil.

When looking for pictures, I try to find one that's already the right size for the notebook cover, and a clear picture is easier to trace. I usually copy them from magazines, but you could also search for images on the internet (check copyright before using). I choose pictures that reflect what I'm going to use the notebook for: the chair notebook is for lists, measurements and quotes; for a shopping-list notebook, I used a shopping trolley; for Christmas gift lists, a Christmas tree was the obvious and easy choice; and for craft ideas I used the chalkboard.

Time taken Under 30 minutes

What we used

- 10 sheets of white A4 paper—I just use recycled photocopying paper
- 1 piece of thin black A4 cardboard
- Scissors
- Interesting picture from a magazine
- Baking paper—any partially transparent paper will work
- Pencil
- White pen
- Sewing machine—mine was threaded with red cotton so that's what I used

What we did

First the preparation

- I cut the ten sheets of white paper and the sheet of black cardboard in half lengthways.
- Once I'd chosen a picture, I put the baking paper over the image and traced over it in pencil.
- I folded the black cardboard in half, placed the baking paper on the front, with the pencil tracing facing the cardboard, then rubbed the back with the pencil to transfer it. The image is reversed using this method.
- Then I carefully drew over the pencil image in white pen.

Now for the construction

■ I stacked the white paper, and folded it in half. My edges are always a bit uneven—you can minimise the unevenness by folding just a few pages at a time.

■ Then I unfolded the stack again and put the black cardboard on top—I made sure the picture was on the outside, right way up.

■ Finally, I sewed a straight machine stitch along the fold crease and trimmed the thread, leaving a bit dangling—I thought it looked cute that way. Then I refolded the stack and my nifty notebook was done.

Variations

■ You could use a gorgeous printed cardboard or paper for the cover instead, or collage the cover.

■ Coloured paper for the pages would be fun—or even multicoloured in one notebook.

■ Get a kid to draw a picture on the cover!

16 Pretty peg dolls

Idea and inspiration

When I was six years old I went to the Henty Field Day with my dad—it's an event showcasing agricultural machinery. It had a really catchy ad that my six-year-old self totally fell for. I'm sure if you're into agricultural machinery the Henty Field Day would be awesome. But the only thing that got me through the utter boredom of the day was a craft stall that sold peg dolls. Dad got me one and I played with it for nine hours. I have had great affection for peg dolls ever since.

Time taken 10 minutes per doll

What we used

- Old-fashioned pegs—the craft store kind
- Black marker pen
- Scraps of matching fabric—some were as small as 5 cm × 10 cm
- Scissors
- Needle and thread

What I did

First the preparation

- I drew hairdos on the pegs with black marker pen, then added their faces. I suggest checking the alignment of the 'legs' before you start drawing— when I made my first doll, I didn't.
- Having decided to run with a black and white theme, I chose some little bits and pieces of fabric—these were offcuts from other projects.

Now for the construction

- For each doll, I just worked the fabric scraps into something that resembled an outfit. A bit of tucking, folding and trimming was required. I mostly made little rectangles that would fit around the doll as either a dress or a skirt, but I also found that little triangles could be wrapped around them too. I didn't worry about finishing edges.
- Once I was happy with the clothes (and they had Lotte's approval!), I stitched them at the back. The clothes move about a bit, but it means we can change their outfits easily when we get tired of them or they get too dirty—these dolls were later dressed in gold pieces. You could add a strip of all-purpose glue at the back if you want them to be more secure.

Variations

- You could make these a lot more detailed if you are so inclined—I might draw on some little boots or shoes next, or stitch a little hat.
- We have also used the same clothing construction method for bigger dolls. (Some days I think I'm just one step away from making myself clothes this way.)

AND THE LITTLE ONE

The little lass was a sort of stylist. She handed me the fabric pieces and approved the final cut. She loves the finished dolls. They are often named after her friends Esme, Matisse and Mimi, who all have dark-haired bobs. She can play with them for ages— not quite nine hours, but ages. It is worth noting that the dolls are very easy to pack for outings and seem to be fond of long train trips.

17 Fascinating flower headband

Idea and inspiration

Today I saw new skinny headbands for sale—three for $2. Bargain! Oh, the possibilities! I intend to decorate all three but this is the first. As soon as we got home I grabbed the ribbon box to see what we could find. I realised I have kept every ribbon that passed through our door. This was followed by the thought, 'I am becoming my mother.'

Time taken 15 minutes—maybe a bit less

What we used
- An old ribbon
- Needle and thread
- Cheap plastic headband

What I did

First the preparation
- I chose a big satin ribbon from the stash; this one was from some wedding anniversary flowers. It was pretty on both sides—which was important, as both sides would be seen—and was also light, shimmery and quite delicate-looking. It was about 60 cm long—even longer would have been better, but I worked with what I had.

Now for the construction
- Along one side of the ribbon, I sewed a simple chunky straight stitch, about 5 mm from the edge, and then slowly gathered up the ribbon. I then kind of moved it around until I liked the shape—the bigger the better. I wanted this one to be really fluffy, so I had to pull the gather very tightly.
- I also stitched the messy ends under the bottom where they won't be seen.
- Finally, I worked out where I would like the flower to sit on the little one's head and stitched it to the headband. I simply sat the flower on top and then sewed around the headband and through the base of the flower. I'm so messy but I did whatever it took to get it on there.
- That was it. Oh so easy.

Variations
- You could attach flowers made this way to badge parts; you could stitch them directly onto clothing or canvas bags. Oh the possibilities!
- I am tempted to make a whole headband of these, so it is like a delicate little floral crown.

AND THE LITTLE ONE
Lotte was quite snuggly the day we made this and happily sat with me and watched the whole process develop. She said, 'That's amazing.' It isn't amazing, but it is nice of her to say so.

18 Yoyo shoes

My childhood next-door neighbour, Aunty Pearlie, had a cushion cover made from these little circles. I adored those little 'puffs' but until this evening I had never made one. They are so cute and easy, I'll certainly be making more. Perhaps one day I'll make my own fascinating cushion cover. (I've since found out the puffs are actually called 'yoyos'. Did everyone else already know that?)

Putting stuff on shoes was something my mum used to do. She was great at decorating them and, as it was the 80s, she would do a bag to match. She painted the shoes, trimmed them and clipped various things to them, mostly clip-on earrings. She also showed me how to clip bows that I made to my shoes.

Time taken 15 minutes

What we used

- Fabric pieces, 10 cm square
- Large tin can, bowl or other round object
- Pencil
- Scissors
- Needle and thread
- 2 paperclips

What I did

First the preparation

- I chose the fabric—this came from the 250-plus quilt squares I cut out when I was pregnant and which I'm still trying to use!
- Using a large tin can (ours had a 9-cm diameter) turned upside down, I traced a circle on the fabric and cut out the circle. I did this twice.

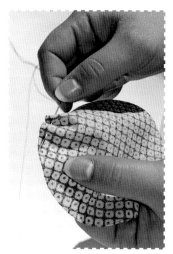

Now for the construction

- It was much easier than I thought—I just sewed a basic straight stitch around the whole circle, about 5 mm from the edge. At the end, I carefully gathered the thread tight to create my yoyo.
- To finish it off, I tied the ends of the thread together.
- Then I repeated the process to create the second yoyo.
- To attach the yoyos to shoes, I decided to just use a paperclip. (I would have used the back of a clip-on earring if I had some, but I don't.) I just sewed the paperclip to the back (flat side) of the yoyo, stitching all around the end of the larger part of the paperclip. This worked, and so far I haven't lost a paperclipped yoyo off a shoe.

Variations

We will certainly be making some bows one day and clipping them onto shoes, and I think I'd quite like to make a big pile of pompoms and attach those too. I'm also on the lookout for big flat clip-on earrings that I can stick buttons onto.

AND THE LITTLE ONE

Lotte stayed around during this project. She helped me pull the thread for the second yoyo and played with bits of fabric while I stitched on the paperclip. She loves the final product and thinks they make her look like she has fairy feet. I definitely want something for my shoes, too!

19 'Little uni' bag

Idea and inspiration

Our daughter named her preschool 'little uni'—not because we are engaged in ridiculous early pressure, but because it's one of the childcare centres at the university I work at and so she said that while I go to 'big uni' she will be at 'little uni'. Anyway, we bought her a small backpack like all the other kids had because we didn't want her to feel out of place. I doubted she would, but just in case. It was a very pink one with pictures of little girls on it—not my style, frankly, but she packed it carefully and wore it proudly. A few days later I picked her up, we caught a bus home and never saw it again. Neither of us seemed to care much. That night we designed and made a new bag together.

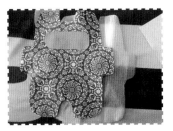

Time taken An hour (or thereabouts)

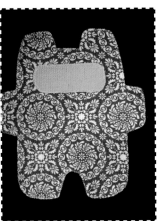

What we used

- Denim for the bag
- Piece of printed fabric for the monster—we started with a 20-cm × 30-cm piece
- Scrap of fabric for his eye area—ours was about 5 cm × 10 cm
- Scissors
- Pencil and paper, for making a template
- Chalk
- Buttons
- Vliesofix (see 'Basic Techniques')—this stuff is the greatest; run out and buy some . . . quick!
- An iron
- Sewing machine
- Ribbon
- Needle and thread

What I did

First the preparation

- We decided on a size—small enough for Lotte to carry over her shoulder and big enough to hold a snack, a drink and some socks (she always carries socks 'in case I get cold'). Admittedly, it was a bit too small—about 25 cm × 30 cm and with hindsight I recommend at least 35 cm × 35 cm. I cut out two pieces of denim for the body of the bag.
- We decided on a design—she asked for a monster. (So much for me thinking that pink with little girls was her style.)
- I drew and cut out a monster template (on a folded piece of light cardboard for symmetry). The little one thought he was sufficiently monster-ish and I thought he was sufficiently easy to sew.

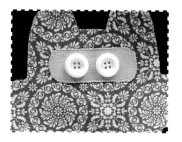

She chose the fabric for the monster from a selection I offered. Using the monster template, I cut out the fabric. We found a scrap of contrasting fabric for the eye area and cut that out from a freehand drawing. Then we tried a few big buttons for his eyes to see which looked best.

Now for the construction

▦ Vliesofix comes with instructions—make sure you ask for them and then follow them in addition to my process.

▦ First, I traced around the monster's body onto some Vliesofix, and did the same for the eye piece. I cut out both pieces of Vliesofix. I ironed the eye piece onto its Vliesofix (protect your iron by placing paper between your iron and fabric), before ironing it onto the fabric for the monster. Then I ironed the monster fabric onto its Vliesofix, followed by ironing it onto the front of one of the denim pieces. More detail of how to do this can be found in the 'Basic techniques' section.

▦ To keep them strong and secure, I simply did a neat, tight zigzag stitch around the monster and the eye piece.

▦ I decided to do a French seam on the bag for both strength (the bag would get a lot of use) and presentation. Details of French seams can also be found in the 'Basic techniques' section.

▦ After turning the bag the right way out, I neatly folded the top to the inside (a double-folded hem is probably best—see 'Basic techniques' again). Then I ironed it in place. You can add a couple of discreet stitches to keep the top flat or hem it (I didn't though).

▦ I worked out how long the ribbon needed to be for the bag to hang over Lotte's shoulders (about 60 cm), then I cut the ribbon and machine-stitched it to the inside of the bag, just over the side seams (I went over it a few times for strength).

▦ Finally, I sewed the buttons onto the monster to make his eyes—placing them somewhere eye-like on the patch, then starting with a knot at the back and using a neat, strong stitch to hold the buttons on.

Variations

▦ This is essentially just a simple tote-bag pattern. You can make them out of anything you like—I have a basic one I made for myself using a vintage tea towel and a ribbon. I also used to make them out of bold fabrics and sell them cheap at uni and festival market stalls when I had some bills to pay.

▦ The monster application method can be used for any fabric. I learnt it when I was twelve and we made cushions in home economics. (I love the words 'home economics'.)

AND THE LITTLE ONE

Impressively, she stayed involved and engaged throughout. She very happily drew with chalk on scraps of denim when I was ironing and sewing. This bag continues to serve Lotte well, and she has never once asked to have a bag like the other kids, possibly because she had so much input into its design. Apparently she still tells people that we made this together, which makes me ridiculously happy and proud.

20 For the love of tangrams

Idea and inspiration

Get ready to be fascinated . . . for hours! When I was a child I had an activity book with instructions on how to make tangrams. I was obsessed! I made a lot of them—though one is actually enough. This uses the same process but I've made it from a picture instead of block colours, so it doubles as a jigsaw puzzle as well. The picture also makes it easier for me to put it back together when we're finished with it—perhaps I've lost some puzzle skills with age.

Time taken A bit less than 30 minutes

What we used

- Cute picture—this is from a damaged storybook
- A4 cardboard—medium thickness (we used a recycled box)
- Pencil
- Ruler
- Scissors—a Stanley knife or box cutter would be better
- Glue stick
- Magnetic tape

What I did

First the preparation

- We settled on a picture that was simple and sweet. We decided on this first so I knew what size to make the tangram. Ours was 16 cm square.
- I cut a square from the cardboard that matched the image size. You can choose any size square to suit your picture, but I recommend having side lengths that are easily divided by four (e.g. 12 cm, 16 cm, 20 cm), as it makes it easier to draw your tangram. My hint for drawing a right-angled square is to use the sides of two books, measure and draw your desired length, and then turn them around and do the other two sides.
- On the cardboard, I drew sixteen even squares by dividing two adjacent sides into four and then creating a grid.
- Using the grid, I drew my tangram shapes (just follow the photo—so much easier than trying to use words!). Of course, you can vary the shapes to suit your picture.

Now for the construction

- I covered the entire blank side of the cardboard with glue, stuck the picture onto it and trimmed the picture to size. Then I left it to dry for a few minutes.
- Following the lines I'd drawn on the cardboard, I cut out the tangrams (I used scissors but I could have used a blade). I repaired any corners that came unstuck while cutting.
- We added strips of magnetic tape to the back so it can live on the fridge.

Variations

- If you are good with a saw, you could make them out of wood and then paint the pieces.
- Instead of a picture, you could use coloured paper. The pieces can be all the same colour, or each piece can be a different colour.

AND THE LITTLE ONE

Lotte absolutely loves the tangram. She has been making amazing shapes and stories—I'm sure there's some seriously good brain development going on. Hearing her three-year-old voice say 'tangram' is rather sweet too.

21 Functional felt tray

Idea and inspiration

This project came about after I went to our new favourite café in Leura in the Blue Mountains and I saw a shop next-door selling leather trays constructed this way. It was so superbly simple, I just had to make one. Theirs was elegant, beautifully constructed and oh-so expensive. Mine is kind of cute, really functional and cost about 50 cents. On further consideration, it isn't that similar at all.

Time taken 15 minutes

What we used

- A4 felt sheet
- Crochet thread
- Big needle

What I did

First the preparation

- I trimmed my felt sheet to create a 20-cm square.
- Because I wanted the stitching to contrast with the felt, I chose a red and white crochet thread. You could choose a matching thread instead.

Now for the construction

- I folded the felt in half to form a triangle. Using a straight hand stitch, I started sewing at the folded edge, 3 cm in from a corner, creating a little triangle in the corner. The further in from the corner that you start the stitching, the deeper the tray will be.
- Then I stitched the opposite corner in the same way.
- I unfolded the felt, and refolded it in a triangle to stitch the other two corners.

Variations

- I really like this. I'm going to make more in different colours and put them around the house. I might invest in nicer, woollen felt, too.
- I'm planning to make quick versions of these trays using thick paper or cardboard, stapled at the corners instead of sewn, to take to picnics and parties.

AND THE LITTLE ONE

As this was done without a lot of planning—I just picked up the bits and made it very quickly—Lotte wasn't involved much at all. She loves it though, and has since asked if she could make one: she plans to use it to hold her 'cash'. So I'm going to give her a big, rather blunt needle and we're going to sew it together. It will be my daughter's first sewing project.

22 An invitation to tea

Idea and inspiration

When we moved to our new home we heard from many sources that we had wonderful neighbours—hooray! We were rather keen to meet them all. Although I was doing pretty well just running into them on the street, it started to rain—a lot—and the random encounters ended. So a tea at our place was planned. I really wanted an image of rain going into a teacup for the invitation and I didn't fancy my chances of finding one in a shop so, of course, I made one. I love this type of card—it's easy, unique and effective—and I've made a few over the years.

Time taken 30 minutes (minus the faffing I did deciding what papers to use)

What we used

- Scrapbooking paper sheets—a gift from someone who knows me very well
- Pencil
- Scissors
- Glue
- Thin white A4 cardboard
- Print store to make copies—or you could use a colour photocopier

What I did

First the preparation

- I had already decided on my design—rain clouds and a teacup. Next I had to choose papers that would match my design. The clouds were easy—blue. The little one rightly pointed out 'but clouds aren't blue they're white'. Blue looks cuter though. I spent far longer than necessary choosing the teacup paper. Of course I returned to my first choice.
- My freehand drawing skills aren't great so I did an online image search for 'teacup drawing' and then drew a bit of a mix of what I found. I drew on the back of the paper (my eventual teacup was the reverse of my drawing). You could also search for an image online, resize it, print it and then trace over it. (Be careful of copyright.) I managed to draw the cloud and raindrops by myself.

Now for the construction

- This was rather easy. I just cut out the shapes and stuck them on the white cardboard. I couldn't cut out the cup handle so I just stuck a bit of paper over that part to create the 'gap'—that was actually a bit tricky, but I just kept trimming until it looked okay. The card design was now done.
- These ones were little postcards rather than the usual folded cards. I took a bit of a shortcut and instead of making twelve by hand, I just popped up to my local print store and they did quality prints for me on slightly heavier card. (You could also use a colour photocopier.) Then I wrote a brief message on the back and they were ready for delivery.

Variations

- I used scrapbooking paper to create the images but in the past I have used newsprint, sheet music, gift-wrap, magazine pages and so on.
- You can make numbers for birthday invitations. I have also pictured balloons, hearts, little cars and monsters—endless options.

AND THE LITTLE ONE

Lotte was a big part of the delivery for this one. She'd never really posted anything before so she got dressed up, put the invitations in a little bag and carried them around to drop in the letterboxes.

P.S. It was a lovely afternoon tea. We really do have amazing, interesting and kind neighbours (who also make some delicious treats). The little one met some new friends so she wants to make more invitations for more parties to make even more friends.

The tea party was also where we met the gorgeous Sorrel who helped with the photos for this book.

23 Quote board

Idea and inspiration

I saw this frame at a re-use centre and immediately thought it would make a great chalkboard. So I paid my few dollars and walked home, pushing the stroller with the frame draped over my shoulders. The day after it was finished, I wrote a quote on it and that theme has just continued. My intention was to change the quotes weekly: that doesn't always happen.

If you don't happen to stumble upon an awesome second-hand frame like I did, then any frame painted black would suffice. (Someone recently told me that this one was originally sold in IKEA.) For the board I used an MDF offcut that a neighbour was throwing away, but you can also go to a hardware store and get a piece cut to size.

Time taken 45 minutes

What we used

- Picture frame
- MDF or any thin sheet of timber
- Pencil
- Saw
- Chalkboard paint
- Paintbrush
- Newspapers—for protecting walls and floors during painting

What I did

First the preparation

- The first step was to cut the timber to size. I placed the frame on the MDF and outlined the inner shape in pencil. It's better to make it bigger than smaller, as you can always cut extra off but you can't add it back on. (I would like to thank my Year 7 textiles teacher for that wisdom—and for 'measure twice cut once' as well.)
- I cut the MDF with a jigsaw, but a handsaw would work too. It was a total mess, but you can't tell from the front because it's covered up by the frame. If you hack at the timber like I did, then just make sure you get the size right.

Now for the construction

- The only significant thing left to do was to paint the board. Lotte and I painted this together. She was only two when we did this, and two-year-olds and black paint are a scary mix—protect your surfaces well!
- Once the paint dried, we put the board in the frame.
- The hardest part of this project was choosing what to write on the board!

Variations

- Chalkboard paint is amazing. I always have some at home. We have painted doors, cupboards, pieces of wood, clipboards, frames, odd little ceramic sculptures, chairs, pieces of cardboard and tables— I should probably stop. I like the option of drawing on it, but I think it is the matte black texture that I find irresistible.

creativity

is

contagious

–

mr einstein

24 Janey socks

Idea and inspiration

My daughter doesn't like wearing socks. This shocks me, as I loved socks as a child and had a great collection—I even won a prize at a school 'crazy sock' day. Surely she should be genetically predisposed to sock loving?

Besides trying to assert parental taste on her, I also need her to wear socks as it gets cold, really cold, here in the mountains. To rectify this situation I resorted to indulging her love of 80s fashion (certainly some parental taste influence there) by making some very 80s-looking socks, which she calls 'Janey socks', after Janey/Sarah Jessica Parker in the movie *Girls Just Want to Have Fun* (we watch the dance-off on YouTube a lot). She recently told me that when we get chickens she will also call one of them Janey.

Time taken Less than 15 minutes

What we used

- Ribbon—at least 50 cm
- Needle and thread
- One pair of plain white socks

What I did

First the preparation

- We chose the ribbons from the gift-wrapping stash and I cut them to the same length—25 cm.

Now for the construction

- Rather than tying it, I folded the first ribbon into a bow so it would sit nicely. I had the needle and thread ready to sew a couple of quick stitches to keep the bow in place.
- Then I just placed the bow at the top of the sock and kept stitching. My stitches looked nice on the outside, but on the inside they were just awful—I may use white thread next time!
- The hardest part was to get the bows looking the same. So I kind of folded the second one over the first to match up the sizes. They were close enough.
- Again, I just did a few stitches to keep the bow in place then sewed it to the second sock.

Variations

When I was little, I decorated socks in so many different ways. I often made frilly bobby socks by gathering a ribbon and then hand stitching it in around the top of the school socks. Later I embroidered DAD on a pair of men's walking socks for Father's Day. I even tried tie-dying a pair of socks once—a total disaster.

AND THE LITTLE ONE

Lotte wrapped herself in ribbons from the ribbon basket, and in between sewing I helped her knot them. She then pretended she was a ribbon lion . . . of course.
Good news is that it worked and she now wears these socks happily. I will have to decorate a lot of socks to keep up the supply, but no complaints about that!

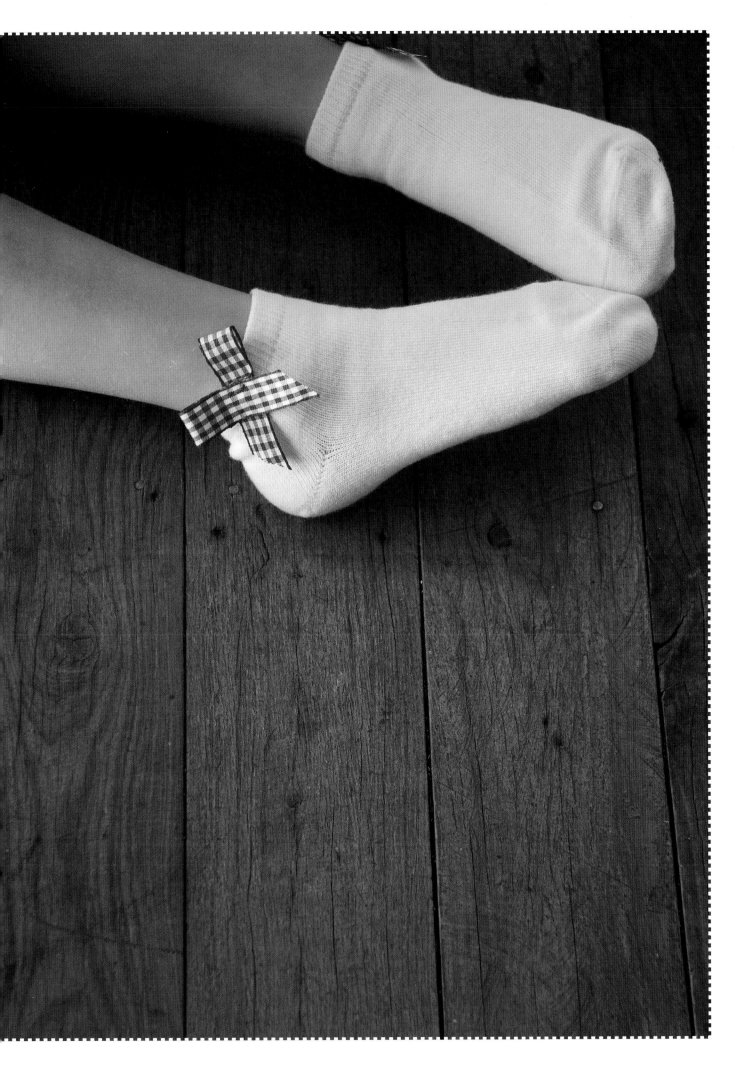

25 Pompom socks

Idea and inspiration

My mum played golf in the 80s. She wore pencil skirts, 50s twin-sets and matching pompom socks. I thought she looked fantastic. The pompoms were both stylish and practical—they stopped her socks slipping into her golf shoes. Clever. I loved those socks so much. If I can be any part of a pompom sock revival, I will be a happy lady. Time to stop reminiscing and start stitching!

Time taken Less than 15 minutes

What we used

- Pompoms
- Ankle socks
- Needle and thread

What I did

First the preparation

- There wasn't really much to do except to buy the socks and dip into my stash of pompoms. If you are feeling really crafty you could hand make little woollen pompoms or, like I did, you could use the little pompoms that you buy in bulk from craft suppliers.

Now for the construction

- I sewed the pompoms carefully onto the back of the socks. The trickiest part was trying to find the centre of the pompom to put some stitches through. I ended up just stitching anywhere and anyhow until it didn't move when I pulled on it. I tried to be neat . . . ish. They will need a lot of washing so the strength of the stitching was important.
- Um . . . that was it. Basic I know, but too good to leave out.

Variations

- Pompom possibilities are surely endless—on brooches, shirts, bags, hats, any knitted clothing . . . As I mentioned in 'Yoyo Shoes' (see p. 52), I'm also going to attach pompoms to paperclips and put them on shoes. I'll use big pompoms and stitch them into a bunch of four or five and then sew the bunch onto the paperclip.
- You could, of course, just use one pompom per sock—or if you love them as much as I do, add even more. I might try a ring of tiny pompoms around the top of the sock; how cute would that be?

AND THE LITTLE ONE

Lotte chose the pompom colours. I was just going to sew one pompom to each sock but she suggested that 'two would be much better'. She spent the next few minutes throwing pompoms all over the room. Then she dutifully picked them up—admittedly I bribed her with her new socks to do so.

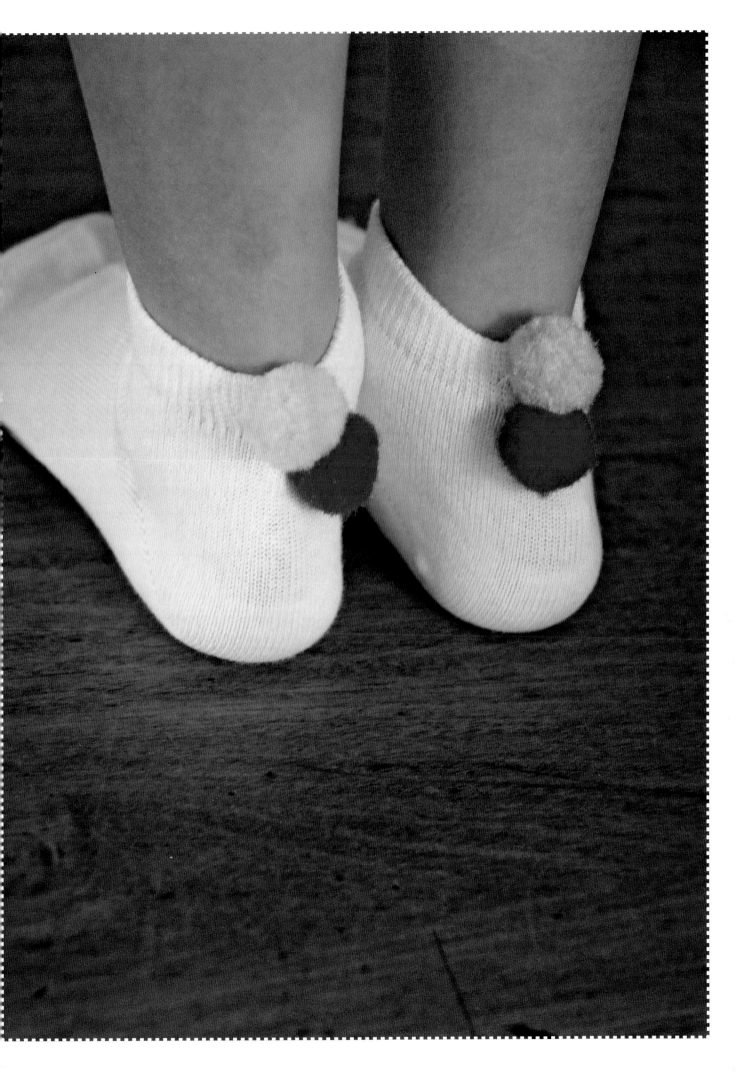

26 Tiny triangle stationery

Idea and inspiration

I had these paint sample cards lying around for about six months. I nabbed them when I was waiting to get paint advice on two different occasions. I still feel bad about not asking (so consider this my very public confession).

I knew that I would cut them into some shape and arrange them somehow—but that was it. So I left the rest up to the little one. I gave her the choice of triangles, circles and squares and left the arrangement up to her (mostly). I think it was nice for her to determine the outcome (mostly).

Colour-copying them to make stationery was actually a long-delayed afterthought. The tiny triangles seemed destined to live their life as a 'fridge piece', until one day I was looking up at them and had a flashback to bright 1980s stationery that I used to send to my penfriends. I used to daydream about designing my own stationery and postage stamps. Now, thanks to my trusty colour-copier, five minutes after the flashback I had fulfilled part one of that dream.

Time taken About 45 minutes

What we used

- Colour sample cards (I had 14)—any coloured card or paper will do
- Pencil
- Ruler
- Scissors
- 1 sheet of white A4 paper
- Glue
- Colour photocopier and paper

What I did

First the preparation

- First, I cut off any logos and print. I played around until I worked out what size triangles matched the colour sample card. I realised I could fit six per card. You can make them as big or small as you want.
- I measured the triangles with a ruler—in hindsight I would make a small template and use that. Then I drew the appropriate lines and cut a couple at once, to save time. This bit was quite fiddly and although Lotte was into it at first—she was ruling lines and so on—she soon got bored and wandered off then started taking photos of me making them. Next time I will prepare the shapes while she sleeps, even though she may miss the minor maths lesson.

Now for the construction

- Once the triangles were all cut, I grabbed the sheet of white paper and we started gluing.
- This was one of the most fun things to make so far. The little one chose a triangle, I put the glue on the back of it and she instructed me where to place it so she could press it down. Obviously older kids can do more of it themselves. I did the smaller neat ones down the bottom (can you tell?).
- Colour-copying the design to make stationery came later—I loved seeing the stack of printed sheets though!

Variations

- These are only limited by imagination—you could cut the coloured cards in different shapes, use them to create neat or random designs, or make them into beautiful overlapping circles.
- You could expand your stationery empire further by making matching envelopes and cards.
- As for the stationery, you can, of course, colour-copy anything. We wrapped some nicely and gave it to Nanna to encourage correspondence.

AND THE LITTLE ONE

As I have mentioned Lotte was the chief decision-maker on this one. While gluing, she said the cutest things like, 'The ones down the bottom are on a train.' She pointed out which ones were her dadda, mumma, nanna, granddad and grandma. She also matched up some triangles so they could 'be friends'. Others triangles apparently liked to be 'by themselves'. If I was gluing them too close, she would speak for the triangle: 'Maybe this one is saying, "Please move over".' We were both fully immersed in this. Sometimes the simple things really are the best—cheesy but true.

27 Big ol' bunting

Idea and inspiration

When I was thirteen I managed to convince my mum to let me make hessian curtains and staple a huge piece on my ceiling. I have had a fondness for this scratchy stuff ever since. Recently I bought three hessian bags really cheaply at a re-use centre and thought I could use them for covering seats. My hubby rightly pointed out that this could be a bit uncomfortable and leave hessian fibres on our bums whenever we sat down. So I put them aside. They lay around for about a month, taking up space, until I did an online search for ideas. Most images were of dog beds, but we don't have a dog. Then I saw a couple of images of hessian bunting—brilliant.

I think every house could do with a bit of bunting somewhere! You can use it for parties, decoration on walls, fences or windows, around tables, or make tiny ones to use as ribbon for gift-wrapping or cake decoration. We had some made out of bright fabrics with pinking-sheared edges hanging over the little one's bed when she was a baby. My rustic hessian version now lives on our fence and seems to be handling our mountains weather so far.

Time taken 30 minutes to an hour, depending on how many triangles you want

What we used
- Hessian bag
- Scissors
- Paper, pencil and ruler, for making a template
- Sewing machine—could also be easily hand-sewn
- Thin rope—I bought 5 metres in a bundle from a cheap variety store
- Large safety pin, for threading the rope

What I did

First the preparation
- I cut the hessian bag along the seams and opened it out. Then I decided how big I wanted my bunting triangles to be—using A4 paper seemed like a good (and convenient) size. You can make the triangles whatever size you like.
- To make a template for the triangles, I folded a piece of A4 paper in half, drew half the triangle along the fold and cut it out while still folded, so that when I unfolded the paper I had a symmetrical triangle. Make sure you include a seam allowance at the base of the triangle (enough to slide the rope through after you have folded and stitched the seam—mine was about 3 cm). I also trimmed the corners off the base so when it was stitched it would be neat.

- Using the template, I cut out all my triangles from the hessian. I just kept going until I had used the whole bag, ending up with fourteen triangles.

Now for the construction

- I bundled up the triangles and took them to the sewing machine (you could hand-sew them easily too).
- Working with one at a time, I folded and hemmed the base of a triangle, leaving enough room for the rope, and sewed a seam using a fairly long straight stitch. I stitched each triangle separately, finishing the seams and trimming thread as I went.
- Once they were done, I just put a safety pin in the end of the rope and threaded it through all the triangles before removing the pin.

Variations

- You can use any type of fabric or paper (obviously, paper ones won't last as long, especially outdoors). I think a string of doilies, stitched directly onto a ribbon, would look nice. (I have started collecting small doilies so I can do this!) You could also have different patterns or colours that match, complement or contrast.
- The triangles can be symmetrical and evenly sized, or they can vary. Instead of triangles, you could use circles, squares, rectangles or a mixture of shapes.

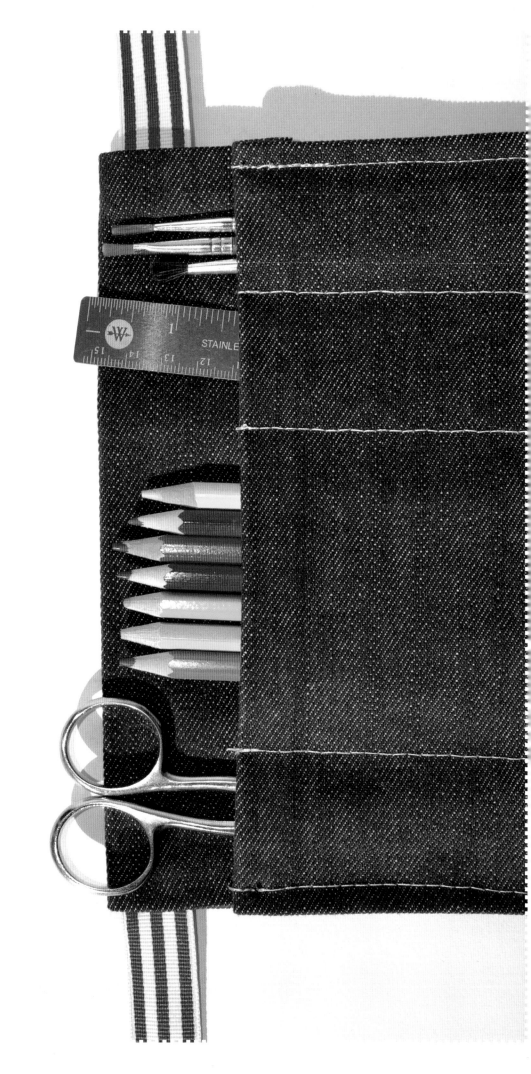

28 For tools and toys

Idea and inspiration

I thought it might be nice to make something a bit more gender-neutral here. The tool-belt idea comes from my dad who, as a builder, spent most of his working days wearing one. I always thought they were such a fantastic invention—though not really appropriate for my workplace . . . Perhaps I could do a craft belt instead!

We made these during a crafternoon with my friend Lee and her daughter Katja. The girls actually ran off to Lotte's room to play dress-ups, leaving Lee and me to chat and craft. Such a lovely way to spend a day.

This belt has since had quite a bit of use. Mostly it holds small toys and often my little one bounds around like a kangaroo with a joey in her pouch.

Time taken Less than 30 minutes

What we used

- Piece of denim—mine was 35 cm × 25 cm so I worked with that (any sturdy fabric could be used)
- An iron
- Pins
- Sewing machine—hand-sewing would work too
- Ribbon—large enough to tie around the recipient (mine was an excessive 1.5 m)

What I did

First the preparation

- You might need to cut your fabric to size—of course, you can make your belt bigger or smaller.
- I folded and ironed a small seam on the two long sides (you can pin them first if you like).

Now for the construction

- I really didn't want to do many seams here so it was all about folding and holding.
- First, I folded a section of the top down on the wrong side (so the raw edge would be hidden), leaving enough room for the ribbon.
- I folded a small seam at the bottom, again to hide the raw edge, then folded that up to meet the previously folded section. (The pictures help that instruction make sense!)
- To hold the sections together, I put a pin on each side and, using a contrasting thread and straight stitch, I sewed the two side seams. Don't sew all the way to the top as you need to leave room for the ribbon to go through the top section.

- Then I put a pin where I wanted the seam for each pocket to be and sewed the seams to make the pockets. I added three seams to make four pockets.
- I threaded a ribbon (my standard red and white stripe) through the top and the belt was ready to wear!

Variations

- I have made this fairly plain but it could certainly be made fancier by using a printed fabric.
- This was done on a crafternoon with my friend Lee, who made one for her daughter—she also used denim but trimmed hers with gorgeous little embroidery flowers.
- Lee also discovered on a road trip that the belt works well hanging on the back of the car seat.

29 Little houses on the hillside

Idea and inspiration

When I was about seven I started regularly drawing pictures of the houses that I would one day own. I included intricate details about the finishes, the floor plan and the various roof gradients (worth noting here that as my dad was a builder this wasn't all that odd). Proof of my continued fondness for houses can be found in the ever-increasing pile of home decor magazines that I reward myself with.

The inspiration for this particular creation was the Malvina Reynolds song 'Little Boxes'. Unaware of the social commentary, my daughter listens intently and asks if she can hear that song again when it's finished. So we hear it often. In a case of wrong song lyrics, she sings 'little houses on the hillside and I love them all the same'.

Time taken 5 minutes per house

What we used

- A4 cardboard—from curtain packaging
- Pencil
- Scissors
- Old sheet music—bought from a re-use centre (also often found at second-hand book stores)
- Glue stick

What I did

First the preparation

- On the piece of cardboard I drew some freehand house shapes. Despite the detailed experiences of my childhood, these ended up being very basic indeed. Then I cut out all the houses from the cardboard.
- I placed the cardboard houses on a piece of sheet music and copied the shapes, adding a couple of centimetres all around the edges for folding over, before cutting them out.

Now for the construction

- I put a strip of glue around the edges of the back of the sheet music, placed the cardboard house on the paper and folded the edges over the cardboard, one side at a time (with neat corners).
- Then I just repeated the gluing for each house. So easy. The glue dried within minutes so we could Blu-Tack them to the wall as soon as we had finished tidying up.

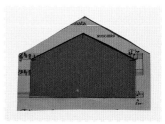

Variations

- I have done more elaborate versions of these involving various house shapes from around the world. The complicated shapes meant that folding over the edges wouldn't work, so I just glued the paper onto the cardboard and cut around it with a blade.
- I think 3D versions would be rather cute—far more structurally challenging though.

AND THE LITTLE ONE

Lotte was very involved in this project. We sang the song (her way). She cut up some scraps of sheet music while I cut out the houses, and helped with the gluing. She also suggested where to put the finished houses— above her toy piano . . . perfect! An unintended consequence is she now understands that sheet music contains the 'instructions' for playing music.

30 The collection box

Idea and inspiration

My sister-in-law posted us a beautiful box filled with handmade chocolates. Oh, how I love chocolate! Anyway, this box is just too cute to get rid of, but I've never been sure what to do with it. I had similar ones when I was child; one I used to sort my family buttons into size or colour groups, and another I used for collections. I had a lot of collections over the years: rocks, erasers, ribbons, nail polish, to name a few. So I thought it would be nice to use this box to introduce the little one to the idea of collecting. Now we just have to find something to start off the collection.

The book is a gorgeous find from an op shop in my hometown—ten damaged books for $1. But after I had started cutting it up, I pulled apart two pages that were stuck together to find that it had belonged to a childhood friend. I felt bad because she may have liked it back, even in its poor state. I am, however, using it to make her something for her baby.

Time taken Less than an hour

What we used

- Pencil, ruler and a 5-cm square scrap of paper—for making a template
- Chocolate box
- Scissors
- Old children's book
- Double-sided tape—bought from my fave re-use store years ago (glue would work too)

What I did

First the preparation

- I measured one square of the tray and made a template that would sit in it.
- Then we chose the pictures (always checking there weren't cuter pictures on the back). I traced around the template and cut out each picture. I arranged the pictures in the tray until we were happy with the layout.
- We also chose a big picture for the top of the box, traced around the lid and cut it out.

Now for the construction

- I simply covered the back of a picture with strips of double-sided tape, trimmed off the excess tape and stuck the picture in the tray. It was fiddly but easy.
- For the top, I just put the tape around the edges on the back of the picture and stuck it to the lid. I admit that I put the picture on sideways and had to trim it! I thought the lid was square. It wasn't.

Variations

- Instead of lots of small, different pictures, I had considered using just one big picture for the tray and cutting it to fit in the squares. If I get another one of these boxes, I think I might line the back with pictures hand-drawn by Lotte.
- I'm thinking of getting a sheet of perspex cut to replace the lid so we can have the box on the wall and see the contents, like mini display shelves.
- Similar ideas could be used for anything with sections.

AND THE LITTLE ONE

Lotte helped me select the pictures, of course. Her favourites were the ones with animals. She also helped me with the layout, which she changed a couple of times while I was sticking the pictures in. The rest of the time she just played with what was left of the book.
I asked her what we should collect and she said a clock, a book, a doll and so on to match each of the pictures—a great idea.

31 Memory garland

My first memory of making a garland was using coloured paper at preschool. This one was largely the result of just wanting to make a garland and looking around for something I could use. I went to my paper drawer and found this damaged book. I bought it in a batch at the same op shop as the book used for 'The Collection Box' project. I thought it might be nice to cut out the pictures of the children and their grandmother and string them together—it triggers many discussions about visits by Nanna and Grandma. I had the sewing machine out and was fairly sure I could stitch them together in one row (I had seen others that seemed to be done that way). It worked.

You can make the circles any size you like, and have as many as you want. I cut out 28. And for the first time in my life I wished I owned a circular cutting tool—I spent at least half an hour just cutting out circles!

Time taken About an hour

What we used

- Old children's book
- Little glass jar for drawing the circles
- Pencil
- Scissors
- Sewing machine

What I did

First the preparation

- I chose the pictures, checking that there was nothing on the back that I preferred.
- With the jar upside-down over the picture, I traced around it. I drew up a few pages at a time then cut them out before starting on the next few pages.
- I arranged the circles in a row until I was happy with the layout, then I stacked the circles, right side up, in the order that I wanted them to appear in the garland.

Now for the construction

- I put the stack within handy reach next to the sewing machine. I took the first circle and straight-stitched across the centre, from left to right, leaving 5 cm at the start for hanging. You can sew top to bottom or left to right, depending on how you intend to hang your garland.
- As I finished the first circle, I had the second one ready so I could continue stitching. I seemed to leave a stitch or two in between the circles without a problem. Just don't overlap them as your garland won't move about freely.
- I continued until all the circles were stitched together. I trimmed the thread, again leaving about 5 cm at the end for hanging.

Variations

- You can make these out of anything you can sew through—gift-wrap, magazines, photos, newspaper, sturdy fabric or even leaves.
- Instead of circles, you could use squares or hearts or a mixture of shapes. Just make a template out of paper or cardboard and trace around it.
- Garlands can be hung on walls, ceilings, doors or windows, and can even be used for gift-wrapping instead of ribbon.

32 Heavenly bonnet

Idea and inspiration

I have had this piece of lace since 1997 when I had a stall selling cute vintage clothes at Glebe markets in Sydney. I bought it from a fabric scrap bin for a couple of dollars. I rolled it up into a tiny roll and it's been in my sewing box ever since. Every once in a while I picked it up, thinking I should trim something with it. But I didn't.

This idea simply came from my daughter putting the lace on her head. It looked like a heavenly little bonnet, so that's what I decided to do with it. And hey, I do love a headband.

Time taken Less than 15 minutes

What we used

- Lace trim—about 1.5 m long
- Thin headband
- Needle and thread

What I did

First the preparation

- Not much prep needed here—I picked up the lace and the headband! I would suggest using a wide piece of lace that's quite stiff (you could starch it to make it firmer); it also needs to have gaps big enough to thread the headband through it. A thin headband allows you to thread it easily.

Now for the construction

- Starting at one end of the lace, I threaded the headband through gaps in the lace until I reached the other end. I fluffed it about until it was evenly gathered.
- Then I sewed a loose straight stitch at the ends of the lace and gathered them to a point, to make it bonnet-like. I then stitched it tightly, and knotted and cut the threads.
- That was it—so easy!

Variations

- You could use any rectangle of medium or heavy fabric by sewing a seam about 1 cm out from one edge and threading the headband through it.
- I can see so many possibilities with this idea! I have a piece of silver fabric from a dress-up costume I made in the 90s that I'm going to use next for a space-girl headband—I'll try using spray adhesive to shape and hold that one up. Frill-necked lizards and flower petals may also feature soon.

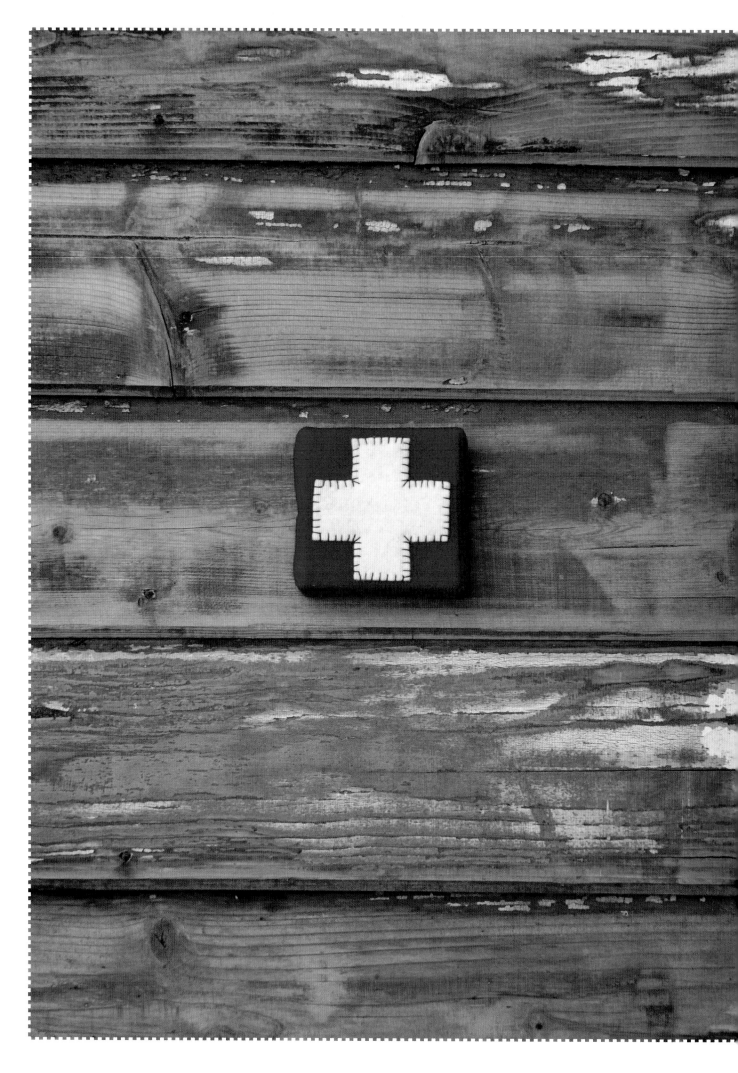

33 Little cross canvas

Idea and inspiration

This project was inspired by a T-shirt belonging to the little one, which was obviously inspired by the Swiss flag (though I must admit the Swiss influence didn't occur to me at first). It is so small because that's the size of the canvas I had. I originally bought the canvas for making a gorgeous handwritten 'L' for Lotte's room. I made it, but it was not gorgeous, so I thought it best to just cover it with something else.

Stretched canvases are available from craft stores, discount stores, artist suppliers or online. I had accidentally bought stick-on white felt, but it actually worked well here—if you're using normal felt, I would secure it using Vliesofix—iron-on double-sided adhesive. I used a staple gun to attach the felt to the back of the canvas but thumbtacks would be fine too.

Time taken Less than 30 minutes

What we used
- Stretched canvas—this one was 10 cm square
- Red A4 felt sheet
- White adhesive A4 felt sheet
- Scissors
- Needle and thread
- Staple gun
- Vliesofix if using non-adhesive white felt

What I did
First the preparation

- I checked that I had enough red felt to cover my canvas and fold over the back on all four sides. I just did this by putting the felt on the canvas and folding it over the back. You could also measure your canvas size, add the depth of the sides, and add another 5 cm all around for folding it over (that would be enough for this small canvas). After working out the size, I cut the red felt into a square.
- Having decided that I wanted the white cross to go very close to the edge, I drew a square 1 cm smaller than my canvas on the back of the white felt. Then I just divided each side by three and drew a grid of nine squares. I cut out the four corner squares and was left with a nice neat cross.

Now for the construction

- Because I was using stick-on white felt, I simply stuck the cross to the centre of my red felt. If I was using normal felt, I'd use Vliesofix.

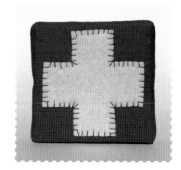

- I decided I wanted a bit more texture, so I blanket-stitched around the edge of the cross—I love that stitch! A straight stitch just a little in from the edge would work well too, I think. Or you don't have to stitch it at all, if you prefer.

- Then I covered the canvas with the red felt, making sure the cross was centred, and folded over the edges at the back (tucking in the corners like I would if gift-wrapping a present). I attached it at the back with a staple gun (see instructions on using a staple gun in 'Basic Techniques').

- To finish off, I trimmed the red felt at the back a bit—nearly too much!— to make it neat.

Variations

- You could make any shape instead of a cross: heart, circle, star, bird, anything you could cut out and sew.

- You can also make them with any fabric—I would suggest using Vliesofix and finishing the edges with a sewing machine zigzag if the fabrics are light or prone to fraying. I keep picturing an 'E' (my initial) in blue on a small floral background—I'm not sure if this is a flashback to something I did in the 1980s or a rather odd false memory.

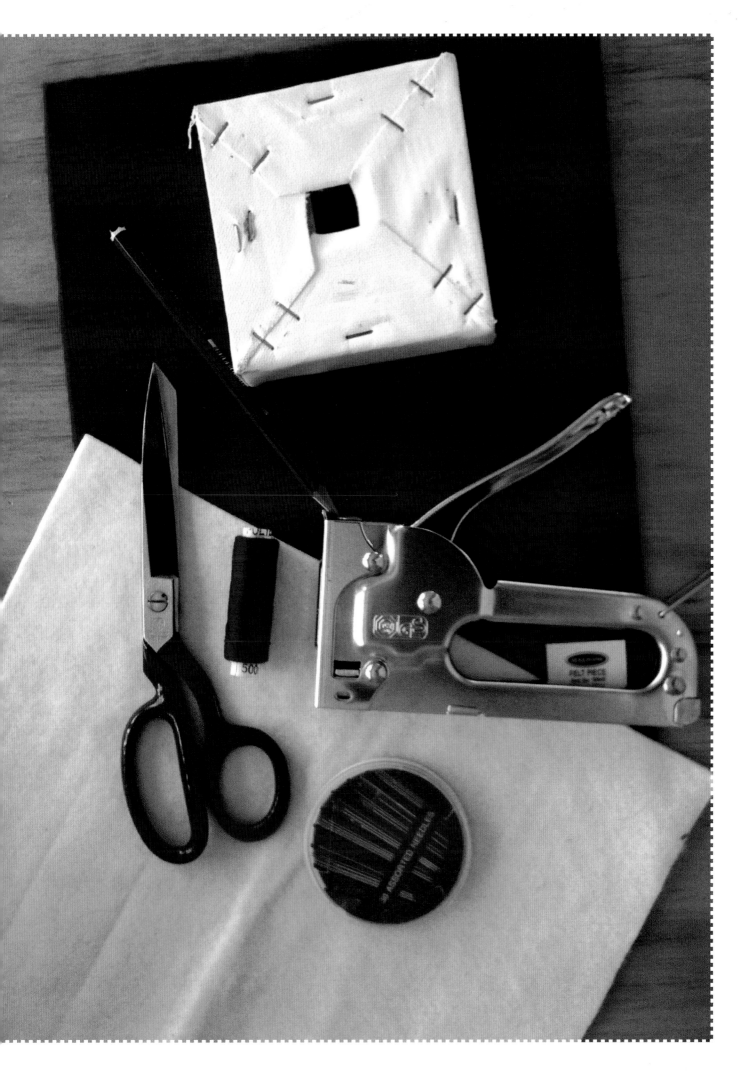

34 Embroidered self-portrait with duck

Idea and inspiration

A while ago my daughter rather unexpectedly drew her first picture of herself as a person—quite well formed, I thought. And, rather oddly, she drew herself with a duck—which actually does look a lot like a duck. I love this picture and kept it on my desk for ages. Then it went missing and I found it days later, all crumpled up—apparently, she wasn't happy with it because she didn't draw eyes. I wanted to do something special with it and thought it might be nice to try embroidery. I used to embroider socks as a kid and I did some cross-stitch in about 1987, but this was my first attempt as a grown-up.

Time taken
I forgot to check but I think it was less than 45 minutes—it depends on what you're embroidering

What we used

- Piece of linen, 60 cm square
- Scissors
- Large embroidery hoop, 42 cm in diameter
- Chalk
- Pencil
- White crochet thread (I actually went to a shop and bought this—it was a discount store though)
- Large needle

What I did

First the preparation

- Photocopy the precious image—I didn't think of that and I have kind of destroyed the original by using it. Yikes!
- I stretched the linen into the hoop and trimmed off the excess at the back. Refer to the 'Beautiful Bunch of Buttons' project for more details.
- Then I transferred the image onto the linen. There are no doubt better ways to do this—but mine worked out okay. I covered the back of the image in white chalk and placed the chalked side on the linen. I lightly traced over the image, leaving a very subtle chalk print on the linen which I then, ever so lightly, drew over in pencil. (I would do this on the back of the linen next time.)

Now for the construction

- I threaded the needle, chose a starting point, knotted the thread at the back of the linen and sewed small straight stitches to form the image. I just kept stitching until I had covered the entire image. When I was done, I finished it off with a knot at the back of the fabric to stop it from coming undone.
- You can see from the back that it's a bit of a mess. I think it looks rather lovely on the front though.

Variations

- I am hooked. I want to embroider lots of things. I went straight on to my next project ('Linen That Loves') and I plan to embroider fabric for cushions too. I'm also going to embroider some gift cards. Even the shoes I'm wearing now could be fancied up with a bit of thread. Maybe I will even do some 'his and hers' towel sets! Maybe not.
- Of course, you could remove the embroidered linen from the hoop and frame it—I just love the look of the hoop.
- I think Lotte's artworks will feature in many future projects too.

35 Linen that loves

I needed to do more embroidery—now! Shortly after finishing the 'Self-portrait with Duck', I remembered the bundles of elegant linen I had just bought at one of my favourite op shops, near my mother-in-law's house in Canberra. Perfect for sewing. My mother-in-law had embroidered some cot sheets with our daughter's name when she was a baby. I decided that a bedtime message would be nice. I thought about 'goodnight' and 'sweet dreams' but settled on the last thing we say to each other when she goes to bed or school or anywhere—'love you'.

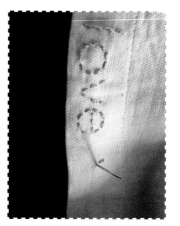

Time taken 15 minutes

What we used

- White bed sheet
- Needle and embroidery thread—I think I got this in a $1 bag of bits that I bought once

What I did

First the preparation

- Once I decided what to write, I decided where to sew it—just to the right of centre. I wanted the embroidery to be visible when the sheets were folded over her blanket. So I folded them just as I would when making her bed to work out where to place my message.

Now for the construction

- I didn't mind the letters being a bit basic or wobbly—if you do, you could write the words in chalk or dressmaker's pencil first (these will wash out).
- After knotting the thread at the back, I started sewing, using a basic straight stitch. A few minutes later I had finished.

Variations

- As I said previously, I want to embroider everything! Pillowcases will be next. I think a little sleeping critter would be nice.
- We've previously decorated sheets by trimming them using pieces of vintage fabric, with handmade pillowcases to match.

AND THE LITTLE ONE

This was so quick. We'd just had friends over and, while I was sewing, Lotte sat down for a snack and milk and by the time she'd finished I was done. As soon as the sheet was embroidered, I put it on her bed and told her what the words mean. She often rests her hand on the words as she falls asleep. So gorgeous.

36 Too-easy doily headband

Idea and inspiration

I grew up in one of those houses that had a doily on every table. (It still does!) I resisted the lure of the doily for some time but recently I have fallen in love with its tiny details and delicateness. The inspiration for this was simple, actually. I took off my plain headband and sat it on the table next to a doily I had just bought (for 20 cents at a garage sale). Two steps away was my little sewing box. I crumpled up the doily a bit and thought it would make a lovely big flower and all it would take was a little gathering. How could I resist?

Time taken 10 minutes

What we used

- Small round doily
- Needle and thread
- Thin headband

What I did

First the preparation

- I did a straight hand stitch around the existing circle of crochet in the centre of the doily. Then I pulled the thread tight—really tight—so the doily gathered up like a flower. I finished it off by tying the thread.

Now for the construction

- At first I thought I would have to stitch the doily flower to the headband. Then I saw that there were little holes in the lace that would be perfect for sliding the headband through. So that was what I did, choosing the holes as close to the stitching as possible to keep it quite firm.
- That was it. See, too easy.

Variations

- I think I will make one of these into a brooch as well—a huge floppy doily-flower brooch.
- You could spray the doily flower with starch or adhesive so it doesn't wobble so much.
- Any circle of fabric would work well, though without the lace holes you may have to do a little stitching to attach it to the headband.

37 Delightful doily collar necklace

Idea and inspiration

Still with the doilies! I remembered that when I was little my mum had this beautiful handmade silver and white lace collar. Recently I asked her if she still had it; not surprisingly, she did. She posted it straight away—she's lovely like that. Lotte is very fond of it so I thought I could make her one of her own (that I might also wear sometimes). The trick was to find a doily that could have the centre quite easily removed. As I have no crocheting skills whatsoever, it required repairs once it was deconstructed. I found this one, and it was pink—perfect.

Time taken 15 minutes

What we used

■ 20-cm round doily bought for 20 cents at a garage sale
■ Scissors
■ 40-cm piece of thin ribbon—also bought second-hand
■ Needle and thread

What I did

First the preparation

■ I very carefully cut out the centre of the doily—being sure to cut only the stitches that joined the lace flowers—leaving me with a circle of lace.
■ Then I cut between two of the lace flowers in the circle. So there was now an opening that I could place around Lotte's neck.
■ I checked it on the little one's neck and this seemed to be a good size. If it was for me, I probably would have added the centre piece to the circle to make the collar a bit bigger.

Now for the construction

■ I stitched two 20-cm lengths of thin ribbon to each end of the collar, ensuring that they were attached to the same 'petal' on each doily flower.
■ When the collar was done, I just placed it around Lotte's neck and tied the ribbon in a bow at the back.
■ You can stitch the edges of doilies to stop them from fraying if you are worried that they might. I would suggest a neat and tiny little zigzag stitch, though I'm sure there are other methods.

Variations

■ You could use actual old collars from shirts to make a collar necklace.
■ You can also make just the collar from a sewing pattern or do a search for ideas online.
■ Or ask your mum!

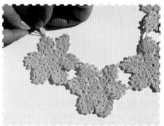

AND THE LITTLE ONE

This was so fast that I didn't even try to engage her much. Lotte did ask what I was doing and I told her it was a special necklace like the one from Nanna. She wanted to know if it would make her look more like a princess or Mary Poppins. I said that would depend on the rest of the outfit, but it could be both. After waiting around for it (while playing with the centre piece), she put it on and commented that it was 'very lovely' and 'could I wear it to sleep tonight?' No.

38 Soft rock paperweight

Idea and inspiration

I often wrap presents in brown paper with string around them—I like the elegant simplicity and earthy look. I was sitting at the table one day and this rock was nearby as it's been my paperweight (it was left here by the previous owners of our house). I'd been using the crochet thread to embroider and without thinking I just started wrapping it around the rock. Hubby saw it and declared that this was one of his favourites. My father-in-law seems to agree.

Like her dad, Lotte seems to really like it. She didn't see me make it but thinks it's pretty and feels nice. I think I'll make another to stay on my desk as this one frequently roams around the house (helped by little hands). Lotte liked it so much we have since started a smooth rock collection that is displayed on our mantelpiece.

Time taken 5 minutes

What we used

- A nice smooth, big rock
- Some crochet thread

What I did

First the preparation

- Um, not really sure that I need many instructions here. This step really just involves finding a rock that is suitable for wrapping and selecting a thread that is both thick enough and contrasts nicely with your chosen rock. You can also use string.

Now for the construction

- I started by doing one wrap of thread and tying a knot in the end at the back to secure it.
- Then I just kept wrapping it. The trick to not having it fall apart was to make the thread tight and ensure it crossed over a lot.
- When I was finished I tied a few knots at the back and trimmed the ends.

Note: The thread came undone once after a lot of handling; I just re-did it. If it happens again, I intend to use clear-drying glue on the back to hold the thread in place. Perhaps I'll even glue a nice piece of felt on the back.

Variations

- I have always had a love of smooth stones—I collected hundreds when I was a child—and mostly I think they are beautiful just as they are. However, I have also seen some appealing things done to them: words written on them, tribal pattern decorations, and simple pictures drawn on them. Children could draw characters on their rocks and use them just as they would use a doll.
- We are in the process of collecting some to make counting stones. The little one is very kinaesthetic and likes to learn by doing things. I think a jar of numbered stones could help her learn to count.

39 My fair lady hat

I bought this plain black hat for $2.50. It's a bit big and falls in my eyes so I kind of walk funny when I wear it. But I still really like it. It was just a bit . . . black. It needed flowers—winter flowers. I was wearing it one day and mentioned to a friend how I would like to decorate it. She said I should and that seemed to be all the motivation I needed. I did it that afternoon. It is a little bit odd but I'm quite happy with it. It reminds me of an Eliza Doolittle hat, before she was a fair lady.

Time taken A bit over 30 minutes

What we used

- Fabric pieces in varied sizes
- Scissors
- Needle and thread
- Hat

What I did

First the preparation

- I chose some scrap pieces of fabric. These were bought by weight from Bird, a wonderful Australian sustainable fabric store—I hadn't known what to do with them before and this was perfect.
- For the flowers, I thought about how big I wanted the petals to be and doubled that to get the width of my fabric. I cut the fabric for the smallest flower to 6 cm wide, the medium flower to 10 cm wide and the largest to 12 cm. The resulting flowers had petal sizes of 3 cm, 5 cm and 6 cm. I didn't worry about the length—I worked with what they already were (which was between 15 cm and 30 cm).

Now for the construction

- I folded the fabric in half lengthways so the print was on the outside and, after tying a sturdy knot at the start, I hand-sewed a loose straight stitch along the raw edge of the fabric.
- Slowly and gradually I pulled the thread tight, gathering the fabric to create the flower shape. Some petals were single layered and others were double layered. I tucked in any obvious fabric edges to hide them and used discreet stitches to hold them.
- Once I was happy with the flower shape, I did a lot of random straight stitches in the centre to hold it in place (avoid making a point though, as this will make it harder to stitch onto the hat).
- I repeated the process to make the other flowers. I thought I would make five or six, but three seemed to be enough.
- Then I simply arranged the flowers on the hat and stitched them on.

Variations

These flowers can be made any size and used almost anywhere (perhaps that is a tad overstated). We have made them for headbands, hair elastics and hair clips. They could be used for brooches and bag decorations too.

40 Golden gift tags

Idea and inspiration

These are so easy I'm reluctant to tell you about the process. They're really charming and rather useful though . . . so I will. I've been making gift tags for as long as I have known what they are. The shape started to change when I saw my first shipping tag. Oh, how beautiful shipping tags are! The process I use to make them pretty much stays the same these days. I recommend making them in batches to have on hand.

These tags can be made using book pages, wallpaper, gift-wrap, even fabric. But I admit that part of their appeal for me is I get to spend ages drinking coffee, eating chocolate and looking through magazines for pictures that would make nice tags (I didn't count this in the time taken). You can use whatever ribbon or string you like, though I wouldn't use anything too wide—our neighbour Karina, an artist, generously gave us this braid when she was moving house . . . it's perfect!

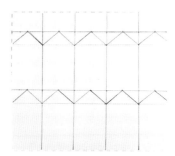

Time taken 30 minutes

What we used

- Magazine pictures
- A4 white cardboard—I always have a ream at home
- Ruler
- Pencil
- Scissors
- Ribbon, 30 cm per tag
- Glue stick
- Hole punch

What I did

First the preparation

- After choosing the pictures, I divided the A4 sheet of cardboard into rectangles that were 10 cm long and 5 cm wide, drawing the lines with a ruler and pencil. Using this measurement I get twelve tags per sheet.
- To create the pointed end, I marked the centre of each tag and also drew a line 2.5 cm in from that edge. Then I used these marks to draw triangles, and cut out the tags.
- An easier way would be to make a gift-tag-shaped template and then just trace it. Why didn't I think of that before?
- I cut the ribbon into roughly 30-cm lengths—you can make them whatever length you like.

Now for the construction

- One at a time, I completely covered the cardboard with glue on the pencilled side and stuck it onto the back of the chosen picture, then I just cut out the picture around the tag—I'm never exactly sure what the tag will look like. If you prefer, you can use the cardboard as a template, place it on the front of your picture, trace around it with pencil then cut out the picture and glue it on.

- When all the pictures were glued on the tags, I left them to dry for just a couple of minutes and then I punched a hole in each tag a suitable distance from the pointed end—I am still surprisingly bad at getting them centred.

- Finally I folded a piece of ribbon in half, popped the folded end through the hole and pulled the rest of the ribbon through the fold. The hardest part of this whole project was getting the braid to sit nicely!

Variations

- The tags can be any size you like and also any shape. I quite like round ones too.

- Animal shapes and hearts might be cute for Lotte's friends.

- I have made more masculine tags with pages from a novel, black cardboard (written on in white pen) and raw-looking string.

AND THE LITTLE ONE

This is another example of my daughter being easily occupied by scissors and paper. This time I made it a little more challenging by getting her to cut shapes and make collages on some cardboard. She loved it. Next time Nanna visited, Lotte showed her how she can make a collage. It has become a bit of a regular bonding activity for them.

41 My heart, my heart, my heart picture

Idea and inspiration

I love repetition. I have seen these kinds of things everywhere. Butterflies feature heavily. I was enchanted by stitched paper when I first saw it in high school. I still think it's beautiful.

In the first hours after our daughter was born I cuddled her and found myself saying, 'You are my heart.' Over time this has extended to me saying to her, 'You are my heart, my heart, my heart,' when I get one of those big bursts of love. Now she is older she sometimes says it to me. She also says that her dada, mumma and 'her own self' all have the same heart. So I wanted to make a picture that had hearts on it. Simple, really.

The white papers came from a sample folder I bought at a re-use centre. I'd had the folder—with its 200 or so paper samples—for about six months and didn't know what to do with it. If you don't have (or want!) that many options to sift through, you can easily do this project with a smaller selection of papers, or even just one paper type.

Time taken 30 minutes

What we used

- White papers—ours were about 8 cm × 5 cm
- Pencil and scrap paper, for making a template—I used a magazine page
- Scissors
- Black paper
- Glue stick
- Sewing machine
- Box frame

What I did

First the preparation

- We made our selection of white paper and decided how many hearts (nine) to feature in the picture.
- I made a heart template by folding some scrap paper in half, drawing half a heart along the fold on one side and cutting it out while still folded. This ensured the heart was symmetrical.
- Using the template to trace around, I drew the nine hearts on the white papers and cut them out.
- I folded each heart down the middle, so I knew where the centre was for stitching and so the hearts would have some depth when displayed.

- I then decided what size to cut my black paper. The box frame I was using already had a mat board that was in the frame. I cut my black cardboard slightly larger than the window in the mat board. If you don't have mat board that suits your purposes, it is fairly inexpensive to take your project and frame to a framing place and ask them to cut you one to suit. I do this a lot.
- Then I arranged the hearts on the black paper so they were nicely spaced, and worked out what size to cut the paper.

Now for the construction
- Starting with the centre heart, I put a strip of glue on the back of the heart, along the middle of the fold, and stuck it to the black paper.
- Then I glued on the other hearts in the same way, making sure I kept them aligned and evenly spaced.
- Once the glue had dried, I straight-stitched each row of hearts along the folds from top to bottom.
- Finally I put the picture in the box frame.

Variations
- There are so many possibilities for this project—you can use any shape, any size, coloured or patterned papers. A contrasting thread would also look great.
- You could also create layers by gluing hearts on top of each other before stitching.
- I have often used the same technique on invitations and cards. Sometimes I stitch one shape in the centre and other times I have used rows of shapes like I did in this project.

AND THE LITTLE ONE

This was done in a lovely evening spent making stuff with the little one and my mum. We occasionally make things when my mum is here, though we more often flick through home decor magazines and chat. Lotte didn't have any specific tasks but we were all happily pottering away on our own things—hers was cutting magazine scraps into many tiny pieces.

42 Simple story scene: Do you think he might eat him?

Idea and inspiration

In our last house we had a beautiful vinyl sticker tree on our daughter's bedroom door. I wanted to have something similar here, but made out of paper—because that's what we had on hand. She said she would like a picture of a cat. So I had visions of creating a fantastic life-size cat sitting outside her room. But every cat I drew was a dud—even the ones I copied from pictures. So plans changed and now a miniature cat stalks a miniature bird sitting in a miniature tree. I really like this one; it is so sweet and simple.

Time taken 30 minutes (to do the successful part)

What we used

- Computer or other picture source
- Scrap paper for making a template—I used newspaper
- Pencil
- Scissors
- Scrapbooking sheets—ours were scraps from a 30-cm square sheet
- Blu-Tack

What I did

First the preparation

- We looked online for a picture of a cat that we both liked. Search terms like 'cat drawing' and 'cat silhouette' worked. I was careful to choose one that was freely available to use (not copyright protected). I then printed it out and cut around the cat shape to make a template. I tried it on various papers to see which one looked best for our paper cat.

Now for the construction

- I traced around the reverse side of the cat image on the back of the scrapbooking paper and cut it out.
- The cat seemed to be looking at something; the little one suggested it was a bird. So the whole process was repeated for a bird.
- For the tree branch, I just did a freehand drawing on the back of some paper and cut it out.
- Once we had our cat, bird and branch, we found a place for them and stuck them to the wall with Blu-Tack.

Variations

- Maybe I'll put some magnetic tape from 'Loving Letters' on the back so they can be moved around on the fridge. Yay!
- You could trace magazine pictures or use storybooks as inspiration as well.

AND THE LITTLE ONE

As I mentioned Lotte was totally involved in the selection of the images. She also seemed very curious about how it would all come together. When we'd finished she asked, 'Do you think the cat might eat the bird?' Of course I explained that the cat just thinks the bird is a wonderful singer and he is listening to him singing.

She continues to be rather fond of the final product. She has shown it to a lot of visitors and moves it around the house quite regularly.

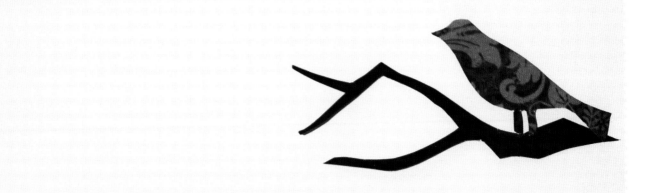

43 The Happy Mr Monster

Idea and inspiration

Three things inspired this:

- Surely I had to make a soft toy.
- I wanted the soft toy to be a basic two-piece pattern (one front and one back).
- Lotte had been having nasty nightmares featuring monsters and I wanted to make her something to outwit them.

Introducing . . . the Happy Mr Monster! The little one named him and we have decided that this monster is so lovely that no monster can be mean in his presence (backed up with passionate declarations about monsters not being real).

This was made on a crafternoon with my friends Lee and Katya (so the 45 minutes it took included sharing of a sewing machine and lots of chatting). Lotte and I chose the fabric for the monster before they arrived. For the front, we selected a patchwork piece that I bought at a half-price sale (the restraint I showed that day was remarkable). For the back, we chose a contrasting fabric—you could use the same fabric for the front and back if you prefer. The contrasting fabric scrap to make his eyes stand out is also optional.

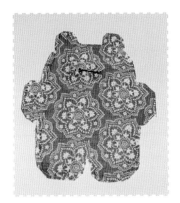

Time taken Less than 45 minutes

What we used

- Fabric for the monster—two 30-cm square pieces
- Fabric scrap for his eye area
- A4 paper and pencil, for making a template
- Scissors
- Buttons for eyes
- Sewing machine
- Needle and thread
- Polyester stuffing

What I did

First the preparation

- After we'd chosen the fabric, I had to create a friendly-looking monster shape (admittedly this looked a bit like a rabbit—and it was almost the same as the monster on the '"Little Uni" Bag'!).
- It was important to have symmetry so I folded A4 paper in half, drew half the shape along the fold and cut it out while it was still folded. You need to include a 1-cm seam allowance all around your monster shape. You can draw your desired shape first and then add another line about 1 cm around that. Then cut along the larger line.

- Using the monster template, I traced the shape onto the front and back fabric pieces and then cut them out.
- I chose some big buttons for eyes, and cut out the contrasting piece of fabric to go behind the eyes.

Now for the construction

- I used a zigzag stitch to sew the eye piece onto the front. You could use Vliesofix to adhere the eye piece to the monster shape first if your fabric is a bit light and flimsy. Then I neatly sewed the buttons on by hand.
- With the right sides of the front and back pieces together, I sewed a basic straight stitch around the edges, with a 1-cm seam allowance. The stitching was quite slow—lots of careful corners. I left about a 6-cm gap on a leg that was big enough for turning the fabric the right way and for stuffing.
- I clipped off the rounded corners on the ears, arms and legs about 3 mm away from the seam, so when I turned it the right way the fabric didn't bunch up.
- Then I turned it the right way out (Lee thought to iron hers so the edges were neat). I filled the rest of the monster with polyester stuffing, being careful to ensure the ears, arms and legs were filled.
- To finish, I did a relatively discreet hand-stitch to close the gap in the leg.

Variations

- There are thousands of 'softies' around. Have a look for ideas online, and if you get right into it you can buy or borrow some very cute books with instructions and patterns.
- I have also used a simple two-piece pattern to make heat bags to pop in the microwave. I use the same approach but instead of buttons I embroider eyes and instead of polyester filling I use raw brown rice. We actually had a gorgeous crafternoon with our friends Mel and Olivia to make little heat-bag ducks this way.

AND THE LITTLE ONE

While we sewed, Lotte and Katja danced, then danced some more, then they dressed up. All was going so (sew—hehe) well that we actually made a few things that day.

The response from my daughter was great. The Happy Mr Monster was well received and appears to be providing much-needed comfort.

44 Cute little cumulonimbus

Idea and inspiration

It is winter here so we thought it might be nice to make it winter for the doll's house too. I have seen a lot of cloud designs lately so that would have also influenced this idea. I actually tried making a cloud in paper first, but it didn't work out. So the easiest option was blue felt. My daughter pointed out (again) that clouds aren't blue, they're white—I know, but a white cloud wouldn't show up on the wall!

I'm starting to think that felt is the most wonderful fabric ever invented (I may be overstating that a bit). I always have some on hand now.

Time taken 30–45 minutes (faster if you use a straight stitch!)

What we used

- Pencil and paper, for making a template
- Scissors
- Blue A4 felt sheet
- Needle and embroidery thread
- Stuffing—we used cottonwool balls
- White pompoms

What I did

First the preparation

- I drew a cloud shape—smaller than the size of my palm—onto paper as I tried to make this in paper first. When that failed I just used it as my template for the felt one. (You could just draw the shape with pencil or chalk onto the felt.) After tracing around my template, I cut out two pieces of felt.

Now for the construction

- I put the two cloud pieces together and stitched almost all the way around the edge. I did a messy blanket stitch—I didn't plan to, I just found myself doing it. In hindsight I would do a simple straight stitch next time—it would be much faster and just as cute.
- When there was just a little gap, I stopped stitching and filled the cloud carefully with cottonwool. The cottonwool balls were Lotte's idea—she just went and got them. Then I finished the stitching.
- I had intended to stop there but it looked a little plain so we added the pompoms.
- First I knotted the end of the thread and added one pompom. Then I knotted the thread again, a little further up, and added another pompom. I stitched the thread to the bottom of the cloud and knotted it.

- I did three threads with two pompoms. They wobble beautifully.
- To finish, I sewed a little loop of thread on the back for hanging—I would do the loop higher next time. I might also use velcro dots to hold it to the wall, when I remember to get some.

Variations

- You could make bigger versions of these and use them as cushions or pillows, though I'd leave off the wobbly pompoms if you do.
- Instead of felt, use normal fabric and cut the edges with pinking shears so they don't fray.
- I think I might make a few more clouds this way, then suspend them all from a stick and hang the stick above her doll's house. One cloud really doesn't reflect the rainy days we've been having.
- You could make the clouds white!

AND THE LITTLE ONE

Lotte happily played with the felt pieces at first. She was interested in what I was doing but most of it was a bit fiddly. After she got the cottonwool balls and I filled the cloud, she used them to make a really big cloud shape on the desk. The felt cloud has been a bit of a hit and certainly gets a lot of attention above the doll's house. When some of her little friends come over, the first thing they do when they go into her room is wobble the pompom raindrops.

45 Cactus pincushion

Idea and inspiration

Yesterday I made the little rain cloud for the doll's house and it occurred to me that the blanket stitch would look cute for the edge of a felt cactus. Pointless, I thought. No, brilliant! I've needed a pincushion for about two years. A cactus pincushion! Everyone needs one of these.

The end result looks a bit like an ill-defined Christmas decoration, but it is kind of cute and certainly functional. You know, it didn't occur to me until I stuck pins in it that the pins are like cactus spikes. Duh!

Time taken 30 minutes (15 if you just straight-stitch it or use a sewing machine)

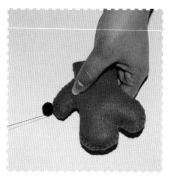

What we used

- Green A4 felt sheet
- Pencil
- Scissors
- Needle and thread
- Cottonwool balls (I really need to buy more stuffing—I suggest using actual stuffing)
- Red pompoms

What I did

First the preparation

- I drew a stereotypical cactus shape on green felt. It took a couple of attempts and my final shape isn't amazing, but it 'does the trick' as my mum would say. My cactus ended up a bit smaller than hand size.
- Then I put two pieces of felt together, with the drawing on top, and cut out the cactus shape—this ensured they were the same.

Now for the construction

- Leaving a gap at the base, I did a basic blanket stitch around the edge.
- I stuffed it with cottonwool balls because I couldn't find anything else—they were making the cactus bulge a bit so I pulled them apart to make them less ball-like.
- Then I just finished stitching across the base to close the gap.
- It was a tad dull so I hand-stitched some little pompoms to represent cactus flowers. I tried to be neat but I just did whatever random stitching it took to get them to stay.

Variations

- You can make a pincushion in any shape you like and use any fabric.
- You could decorate the cactus with little fabric flowers instead of pompoms.
- I used to have a cute little mouse pincushion that sat on a wrist strap when I was sewing. I think I could use another like that so I might make a smaller cactus and stitch a bit of elastic on the back for the wrist strap.

46 Award winner

Idea and inspiration

Lotte saw a picture of a girl wearing an award rosette in a magazine and asked if I could make her one. Of course. I used to make many variations of these when I was young so it wasn't really a stretch. She quickly forgot about it though, so I waited until she was asleep that night and made one. Then, when she had been rather good the next day, I gave it to her in a blatant attempt to condition her to be well behaved.

Time taken About 20 minutes

What we used

■ Broad ribbon for the top—about 1 m
■ Thinner ribbon for the bottom—about 20 cm
■ An iron
■ Big button
■ Needle and thread
■ Big safety pin

First the preparation

■ My gift ribbon stash was getting low at this point so that made my choice easier. Ribbons about 5–7 cm wide work well for the top and around 1–2 cm wide for the bottom piece.
■ I ironed the ribbons flat and chose a big button that would match.

Now for the construction

■ I sewed a broad straight stitch along one long side of the big ribbon. (I love stripes and checks because they give me a straight line to work with.) I also stitched the short ends of the ribbon as they looked like they would fray. This was just included in the broad stitch of the gathering.
■ Next I gathered the ribbon tightly and just wiggled it around until it looked like a rosette. Then I securely knotted the end and trimmed any threads.
■ Once I was happy with it, I added a few random stitches around the centre to keep it in place.
■ I neatly stitched the button in the centre—the thread I used for the ribbon contrasted with the button nicely.
■ To make it look more like an award rosette and less like a flower, I folded the thinner ribbon in half, creating an appropriate angle. I stitched it on the back of the rosette, leaving a loop at the top that was big enough to slide the safety pin through, and then I trimmed the ends.

Variations

You could make tiny versions of these and glue them onto hair clips; offer one to each kid at birthday parties, perhaps with their name or initials on them; or make them in red and green for Christmas decorations.

47 Pomander balls

Idea and inspiration

Now, I thought everyone knew what pomander balls were and how to make them. So I had no intention of putting them in here. Turns out, that's not the case. We invited our neighbours over for afternoon tea today and there was quite a bit of discussion about them. I also discovered that making these could keep older children occupied for almost an hour—after which a gorgeous eight-year-old lass went home with a bag of cloves to complete her ball later.

I love making these. The smell is incredible and the process is so meditative. I particularly enjoy making them while drinking tea at the end of the day.

Time taken 30 minutes—but it depends on the size of your fruit, your dexterity and focus.

What we used

- Tiny organic mandarins—because our gorgeous friend Stella had just given us some (they're usually made with oranges though)
- Clove buds—lots of clove buds

What I did

First the preparation

- Not much is required. I typically choose the smallest piece of fruit and put a pile of cloves in a bowl. I also put a little empty bowl nearby to dispose of the clove buds that aren't spiky enough to push into the fruit.

Now for the construction

- When I was really young, it would take me days to make one of these! Over the years I have developed a system for pushing the cloves in and now I always do them the same way.
- I start with a big circle of cloves around the centre (from the top to the bottom); this 'halves' the fruit. I add another circle across the first, to make 'quarters'. Then I just fill in one section at a time, doing rows as I go.
- I make sure I have small gaps between the cloves so when the fruit dries out I'm left with a solid ball of cloves rather than a partly mouldy mess.

Variations

- These are in bowls at our house at the moment but I used to attach ribbon to them with pins and hang them in my room. I'm going to do the same thing with the next batch and pin them to the back of the wardrobe doors (so they don't actually touch the clothes).
- Mr Muldoon has suggested I make some for the car. Oh, yes! Not quite as cool as fluffy dice hanging from the rear-view mirror but better than the smell of wet towels after the pool.

AND THE LITTLE ONE

After the neighbourhood tea party I saw Lotte putting cloves into a mandarin that one of the older kids had made holes in. So since then I have made holes in the fruit using a skewer and she fills them in with cloves. About twenty holes at a time is enough for her——we then come back to it the next day. (I end up finishing them when the fruit starts to look a bit shrivelled.)

48 Picture pegs

Idea and inspiration

Wooden pegs are just so lovely. About ten years ago I saw a picture of a peg stuck to a wall to hold notes. It was so practical, yet charming. Lately I've seen a few decorated versions at stationery suppliers, but none were quite right for our house. So I decided to adorn my own.

These were so great to make. I actually started making them with the little one—I thought we could make up to five—but I couldn't stop! Mr Muldoon read her to sleep so I could keep going; I was totally absorbed by the process.

I completely adore the mix of patterns and textures of the finished pegs. (For these I used an issue of *Frankie* magazine—mentioned by name because it has gorgeous matte pictures on thick paper in colours that are perfect for our house.) They are serving various roles around our home—holding up artworks, shopping lists, to-do lists, quotes, inspirational pics and thank you cards. They are also used like paperclips to hold pages together.

Time taken 5 minutes per peg (but it really depends on how long you search for the pictures)

What we used

- Wooden pegs—I bought a new pack at our local supermarket especially for this project
- Pencil
- Scissors
- Magazine pictures
- Glue stick
- Blu-Tack, removable velcro and magnetic strips (cut from a plumber's ad)

What I did

First the preparation

- Working on one peg at a time, I chose a picture that I liked, checking that there was nothing better on the other side of the page. Then I put the peg on the picture and traced around it.
- I cut just inside the line I had drawn—the cutting was very careful and accurate.

Now for the construction

- I wanted the spring to be exposed so I placed the picture on the peg and created a little crease with my fingernail where the top of the spring was, before cutting the picture at the crease.
- I covered the back of the paper with glue and carefully placed it onto the peg, then I glued the bottom section the same way and trimmed the end of the paper.

- I repeated the process for each peg.
- To attach the pegs to walls, doors, fridges and so on, I used Blu-Tack, removable velcro picture-hanging strips (cut to size) and strips of magnet stuck onto the back of the peg.

Variations

- You can cover the pegs with anything you like—photos, sheet music, newspaper, coloured paper or gift-wrap.
- You could just let kids colour them in with coloured marker pens.
- You could also stick things on the ends, such as buttons, pompoms or even little plastic animals.
- Instead of covering them with paper, you could paint the pegs (little ones would enjoy that).

AND THE LITTLE ONE

To my surprise Lotte really joined in with this project. She watched what I did then started doing the same thing by herself, choosing her own pictures and tracing around them—very capably. I cut the pictures for her (I didn't cut the spring section in hers) and she glued them on, aligning the ends beautifully. After making three, she said, 'That's enough now.' (I made 30!) The ones she made are on her walls holding up pictures she chose from the same magazine.

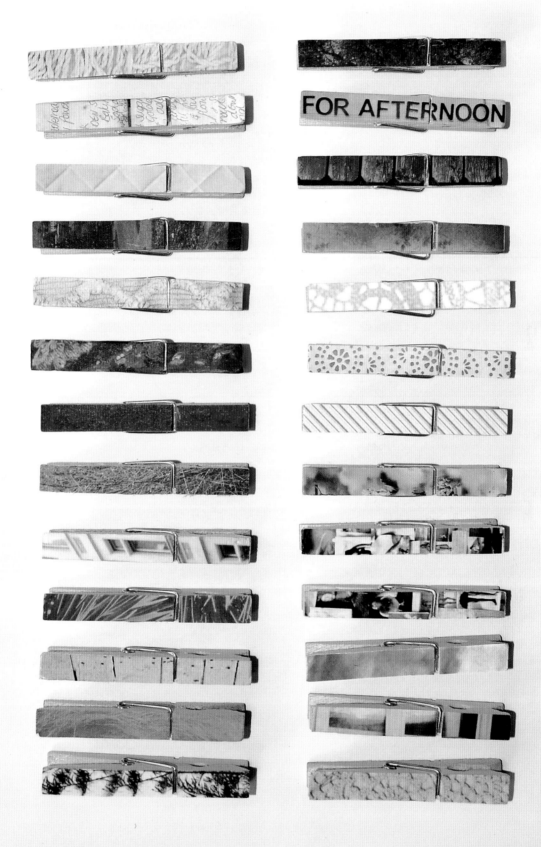

FOR AFTERNOON

49 Tacky babies

Idea and inspiration

While I like the beauty of a brass thumbtack, I started to think it would be nice to have something cute stuck to them. I settled on using these tiny plastic babies that our super-creative friends Pauline and Sunday sent to us. They are bizarre little things. These tacks now hold my to-do lists and make me smile, partly because they remind me of treasured friends but also because there are small babies holding up my lists. They also look very cute holding up this picture of Mr Muldoon having his first haircut. I recently ordered more babies.

Time taken 15 minutes to do a batch (not including drying time)

What we used

- Plastic babies—you can get them at some toy stores, discount stores or online
- All-purpose glue—I like thick glue that is white and dries clear
- Packet of thumbtacks—the flatter the top, the better
- Cotton buds—if you make as much mess with glue as I do

What I did

First the preparation

- I did a test run to see how much glue is enough to hold the baby securely to the thumbtack without spilling over the sides. A small dollop to cover most of the thumbtack seemed to work.
- Then I got the babies ready, placing them in rows upside-down on paper—I did one batch of eight at a time.

Now for the construction

- I put the tested amount of glue on the back of a baby and nestled the tack securely in the glue. They seemed to stay put without me holding them in place.
- The cotton buds were used for cleaning any glue spillage from the sides of the thumbtack. (There was a bit of this!)
- Then I glued the next baby, and so on, until they were all done. I left them to dry overnight.

Variations

- Anything small that can handle the force of being pushed and pulled will work. I think vintage buttons or Scrabble tiles would certainly look more elegant—next time, perhaps.
- You can use the same principle to attach small things to hair clips and fridge magnets. I have also used superglue to attach things to paperclips, but you have to hold it while it sets.

AND THE LITTLE ONE

There were extra babies for Lotte to play with while I glued. She made a slippery dip for them out of a banana. Her comment when the tacks were done was 'These are really cute, are they for my drawings?' They are now.

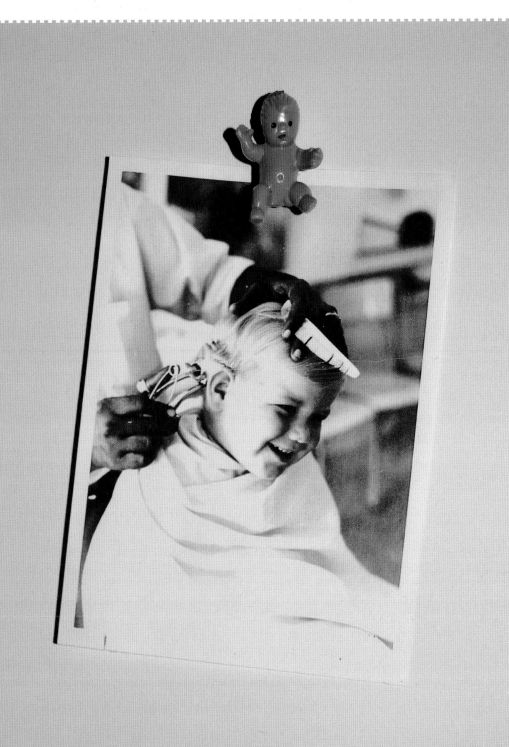

50 Sweet silhouette

Idea and inspiration

When I was five we made these in class for the school fete. The idea was that we created silhouettes of our little heads and then our parents bought them for a few dollars. It was my first school fete and the first thing I made so I was rather excited. That excitement turned to devastation when I got there and they had sold my head to someone else! What? Why? I recovered by telling myself we could make another one at home. We didn't though . . . until now.

Time taken 30 minutes

What we used

- 2 sheets of white A4 paper—quite thick
- Blu-Tack
- Wall
- Desk lamp
- Pencil
- Digital camera and computer—if the silhouette method gets too hard (which is what happened to us)
- Scissors
- A4 black paper—quite thick
- Glue stick
- A4 box frame

What I did

First the preparation

- I stuck a piece of white paper to a wall at the little one's head height, using Blu-Tack. Then we shone a lamp onto the paper (fairly close—ours was about 1 m away).
- We got Lotte to stand in front of the lamp so the silhouette of her face was on the white paper.
- I tried drawing around the silhouette in pencil but she wriggled too much—while protesting 'I can't stay still!'—so we ended up taking a photo of her side-on, enlarging it, printing it and then tracing over that.

Now for the construction

- Once we finally had the silhouette and I was happy with it, I cut out the shape and used that as a template.
- I tried heaps of silhouettes on different papers and tested them with different backgrounds but none of them worked as well as plain white on plain black, so ultimately that was what I used.
- After working out where I wanted the silhouette to be, I glued the silhouette on the edge of the black paper. I then popped it into an A4 box frame.

Variations

- You might have more success than I did with different colours or patterned papers. I quite like the idea of a black silhouette on a page of text, and I haven't given up on it yet.
- You could trace around a whole head and use it as an outline for embroidery. You could even appliqué the silhouette onto a cushion.

51 Cloud ear elephant badge

Idea and inspiration

This was inspired by a gift to our daughter from my sister. We went and did some touristy stuff around town and at a puppet store Lotte eagerly carried around a little box of wooden animal shapes (rather than any of the gorgeous-coloured, costumed puppets). I tend not to give in to impromptu purchase demands, even when I am really tempted, and so on our way out she put it back. Moments later my sister emerged with said wooden animals—so lovely. We have made lots of things with them but I think these are my favourites.

If you don't have a sister who has given you an awesome box of wooden animals, you might find them in craft stores or online. You could also trace shapes onto thick cardboard (such as a box), using cookie cutters or pictures copied from books, magazines or the internet, or draw the shapes yourself if you're handy with a pencil (which I'm not).

Time taken 15 minutes once you have decided on your picture
(not including drying time)

What we used

- A wooden animal shape
- Magazine picture
- Glue stick
- Box cutter or Stanley knife
- Craft glue
- A badge part—available cheap from craft stores

What I did

First the preparation

- Lotte and I sat down and looked for pretty pictures in magazines—clouds, trees and so on. You could also use gift-wrap or any coloured or patterned paper.
- We both roughly cut out a few images (we actually made three badges in this session), then we chose our animal shape.

Now for the construction

- We covered the front of the elephant with glue—we just used a normal glue stick (the little coloured blob is from Lotte drawing on the elephant previously).
- Then I put the elephant onto the back of the image, paying attention to exactly what was on the other side—it was tricky to line it all up. I should admit that I didn't mean for the elephant to have a cloud for an ear but I think it's why the image works so well.

- With the picture side face down, I used a box cutter to trim the shape.
- You could just trace the animal onto the front and then cut within the pencil line as someone with more common sense than myself has since pointed out. That would certainly make positioning easier!
- I glued the badge part onto the back of the elephant using craft glue, we let it dry overnight and the badge was ready to wear.

Note: These badges tend to go on our bags rather than our bodies. Because they are just covered in paper, they wouldn't handle too much damage.

Variations

- These could also be very cute fridge magnets—just replace the badge part with adhesive magnetic tape or squares.
- And possibly even bulky necklace pendants. You could drill a hole or superglue a small circle at the top of the back to thread a ribbon or string through.
- You could use other shapes besides animals, of course—hearts, cars or monsters would be cute.
- You could varnish them to make them more durable.

AND THE LITTLE ONE

Lotte was involved throughout: selecting the images and helping with the gluing. She isn't up to using sharp blades yet so I did that part. When I was cutting, she played with the other animals and we talked about where they live and what noises they make. We couldn't work out what noise a giraffe made so we were momentarily distracted looking up giraffe noise on YouTube and then trying to mimic it.

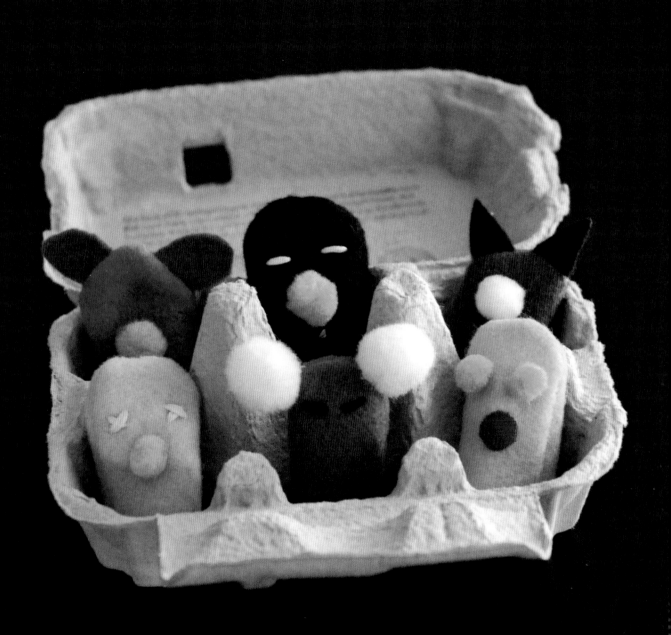

52 Felt folk finger puppets

Idea and inspiration

No great flashes of insight here, I simply wanted to make finger puppets—really easy finger puppets—with the little one. These are the result! They are actually way cuter than I expected them to be.

The egg carton idea seems to have been some kind of implicit memory—my faulty brain thought I had invented it, but I have since seen lots of toys (including felt ones) displayed this way.

Time taken 10 minutes each

What we used

- Pencil and paper, for making a template
- Scissors
- Coloured felt from A4 sheets and offcuts
- Pen or marker
- Embroidery thread
- Sewing machine—hand-stitching would be easy, though
- Pompoms
- Egg carton

What I did

First the preparation

- I traced around Lotte's middle and index fingers onto a piece of paper, adding enough space for the width of her two fingers and a small seam. I cut it out and this was my template for all the puppets.
- Lotte chose the felt colours. I put the template on a piece of felt and drew around it. Then I put the first piece on another piece the same colour and cut the two together so that they were the same.

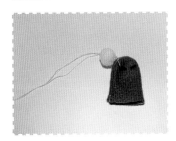

Now for the construction

- First, I embroidered the eyes or mouth or any other feature—the pompoms were done later because they were bulky.
- To create ears, I cut two ear shapes out of felt and placed them, with the points facing down, at the top of one piece of felt, before putting the other piece of felt on top. (Make sure the felt pieces are right sides together.)
- With the felt pieces right sides together, I sewed a basic straight-stitch seam really close to the edge around the sides and top—I used a sewing machine but you can do this by hand.
- Then I turned it the right way out.

- Finally I attached pompoms as desired, sewing them on by hand by roughly threading through the centre of the pompom and then back through the felt.
- I repeated the process five more times—you could do it eleven more times if you feel like filling a one-dozen-egg carton.

Variations

- There are just too many to list for both the finger puppet and the egg carton! No doubt most of us have made things out of both at school. Kids' craft books are full of them.
- You could try making various animal shapes by adding wings or legs or different ears. You could get the kids to draw little finger-puppet faces.
- I am going to try making a hand puppet this way too.

AND THE LITTLE ONE

Lotte was really involved in the design of these. After she chose the felt colours, I said the puppets could have two features each—eyes and ears, or eyes and nose, and so on. She then decided on the features and whether we would stitch them or use pompoms. I think she made really cute choices. I particularly like the blue one with the white pompom ears. The finger puppets are definitely some of her favourite toys.

ACKNOWLEDGEMENTS

Lotte May, thank you for making every day amazing.

Thank you Mum. I couldn't have made this book (or this life) without your constant support and your creative parenting. Love you.

Dad—Don Henry Ferdinand Augustus Charles Wentworth Wells—thank you for fearlessly letting me hammer and saw and glue when I was small. I wish you had met our little lass and been able to teach her to do the same.

Thank you Mr Muldoon for your faith in me and my creative adventures. This is all possible because of you.

To all my gorgeous, creative and supportive friends—you have been so generous with your time, your talents and even your children. I am ridiculously fortunate to have such friends.

Thank you to the wonderful folk at Allen & Unwin—I'm so grateful to you for your patience and generosity.

Zoe Lalancette and Sorrel Hanemann-Fayers, you can never be thanked enough for your beautiful photographs and the many wonderful days we spent taking them.

MEASUREMENT CONVERSION TABLE

We've used metric measurements—millimetres, centimetres and metres—throughout this book. Converting these units to inches can be tricky, so we've worked out some approximate imperial measurements here.

We also use the standard page size 'A4' to describe sheets of paper, felt and other materials. An A4 page is 210 mm × 297 mm (8 ⅜ in × 11 ¾ in). For comparison, the letter paper size commonly used in North America (8 ½ in × 11 in) is roughly 6 mm (¼ in) wider and 18 mm (¾ in) shorter than A4.

METRIC	IMPERIAL
1 mm	¹⁄₁₆ in
3 mm	⅛ in
5 mm	¹³⁄₁₆ in
1 cm	⅜ in
2 cm	¾ in
3 cm	1⅛ in
4 cm	1⅝ in
5 cm	2 in
6 cm	2⅜ in
7 cm	2¼ in
8 cm	3⅛ in
9 cm	3½ in
10 cm	4 in
12 cm	4¾ in
15 cm	5⅞ in
16 cm	6¼ in
20 cm	7⅞ in
21 cm	8¼ in
25 cm	9⅞ in
26 cm	10¼ in
30 cm	11⅞ in
35 cm	13¾ in
40 cm	15¾ in
42 cm	16½ in
45 cm	17¾ in
50 cm	19⅝ in
53 cm	20⅞ in
55 cm	21⅝ in
60 cm	23⅝ in
70 cm	27½ in
85 cm	33½ in
1 m	39⅜ in
1.5 m	59 in
5 m	196⅞ in